Child Care and Protection

Law and Practice

Available titles in this series include:

Agricultural Tenancies

Angela Sydenham

Change of Name

Nasreen Pearce

Charities and Not-for-Profit Entities

Cecile Gillard

Debt Recovery in the Courts

John Kruse

Partnership and LLP Law

Elspeth Berry

Personal Injury Litigation

Gordon Exall

Procedure in Civil Courts and Tribunals

John Bowers QC and Eleena Misra

Residential Tenancies

Richard Colbey and Niamh O'Brien

Termination of Employment

John Bowers QC and Carol Davis

Wildy Practice Guides

Child Care and Protection
Law and Practice

Barbara Mitchels (Editor) with
Julie Doughty, Helen James
and Safda Mahmood

Fifth Edition

Wildy, Simmonds and Hill Publishing

Contains public sector information licensed under the Open Government
Licence v1.0

ISBN: 9780854901135

British Library Cataloguing in Publication Data

A catalogue record for this book is available from the British Library

This edition published in 2013 by

Wildy, Simmonds & Hill Publishing
58 Carey Street
London WC2A 2JF
England
www.wildy.com

Typeset by Cornubia Press Ltd, Bristol.
Printed in Great Britain by CPI Antony Rowe,
Chippenham, Wiltshire.

FSC
www.fsc.org
MIX
Paper from
responsible sources
FSC® C013604

Preface

Helen and I are delighted to welcome Dr Julie Doughty from Cardiff University and Safda Mahmood, Children Panel solicitor, as our new co-authors in this fifth edition of the book.

We have always felt that the strengths of this book are practicality, accessibility and strong roots in practice. Safda Mahmood is an experienced Children Panel solicitor in the West Midlands. He also runs training courses and CPD for members of the Law Society's Children Panel. Julie Doughty has practice experience as a former solicitor and guardian ad litem panel manager, and currently she is a lecturer in law at Cardiff University. Julie writes widely in journals on child law topics and is the Editor of *Seen and Heard*, the journal of NAGALRO (Professional Association for Children's Guardians, Family Court Advisers and Independent Social Workers). Julie and Safda are an impressive team – together they provide a unique combination of academic and research information and practice experience in child protection which has added fresh dimensions to the new edition of this book.

Helen is a Children and Family Court Advisory and Support Service (CAFCASS) children's guardian and an independent social work consultant with a wide range of practice experience. She also now has an exciting new role as Director of Family Practice Contact Services, an agency delivering contact and Family Support work services across the UK.

I recently retired from practice as solicitor, but continue to enjoy my 'other life' as a psychotherapist and Director of Watershed Counselling Service in Devon, bringing together these dual roles in a new venture, *Therapy Law*, providing consultancy, lectures and CPD workshops. In this new fifth edition of the book, the active practitioners, Helen, Julie and Safda have updated the book content, and I have an editorial role.

Child care and protection in England is a vast and dynamic area of law and practice. We cannot cover everything here, but this book provides an overview and practical guide through the maze of the Children Act 1989 and subsequent child protection legislation, guidance and case law. Since the last edition in 2009 there have been significant developments in legislation and practice. This edition covers new material, including the Family Court Rules 2010, other recent subsidiary legislation, guidance and Practice Directions, new case law and the impact of the *Public Law Outline* (PLO).

The law in this book is up to date as at 21 June 2012. Practitioners will need to watch out for further changes in legislation, rules and guidance. Inter-agency co-operation in child protection practice in England is currently based upon the revised edition of *Working Together to Safeguard Children, A guide to inter-agency working to safeguard and promote the welfare of children* (DCSF, 2010), and Tim Loughton, the Children's Minister, is committed to review the current version, which is a long and comprehensive document, to shorten and simplify it. This is currently subject to consultation by the Department of Education. It is also possible that the time frame for hearings in care cases will be further reduced, perhaps to 26 weeks, and the Family Justice Council is currently revising the standards for experts. If any or all of these happen, we can expect concomitant changes to the Family Procedure Rules 2010, which will certainly be affected if clause 17 of the Crime and Courts Bill 2012 is passed, creating a single Family Court as recommended in clause 17 of the *Family Justice Review Final Report* (Ministry of Justice, 2011). The Child Protection Register (CPR) was thought to have been abolished in April 2008 in favour of Child Protection Plans (see Chapter 4), but the CPR certainly continues to exist in Scotland and in Wales, and researchers at Queen's University Belfast found that on 31 March 2011, 42,330 children were stated to be on the Child Protection Register in England.

In the last edition in 2009, we feared that the financial constraints and the loss of expertise would have an adverse impact on child protection applications in the courts, but now, in the aftermath of the tragic death of baby Peter Connelly, for the first time, care applications in England are reported to have exceeded 10,000 in a single year, see the report at www.cafcass.gov.uk. However, with an increase in caseload and a decrease in resources, we continue to be concerned. The Association of Lawyers for Children and NAGALRO, supported by the courts, have campaigned for an increase in public funding resources, but the funding situation today remains complex and difficult. The availability of Independent Social Workers as expert witnesses is currently compromised. The Legal Services Commission (LSC) does not appear to recognise the importance of the use of the expertise of Independent Social Workers, and has in consequence imposed a fee cap on their hourly rate in line with the rate paid to CAFCASS's self-employed contractors. This fee limitation has been widely criticised by Independent Social Workers and has resulted in a significant loss of expertise to the courts. The instruction of such professionals is in future likely to prove increasingly problematic. We hope that the research of Dr Julia Brophy et al (2012) on the added value of ISW reports in complex cases will help to make the LSC reconsider.

From April 2012, the Family Division is piloting a new case management system designed to track public law cases in the family courts, and to provide a range of statistical information which it is hoped will assist courts and professionals in effective listing, avoidance of delays and completion of cases where possible in the interests of the child, within the 26-week target. Mr Justice Ryder is in charge of the Family Justice Modernisation Programme, and we look forward with interest to his innovations; for information, see the updates at www.judiciary.gov.uk.

The Legal Aid, Sentencing and Punishment of Offenders Act 2012 removes from the scope of public funding most private law family cases (with exceptions for those involving child abuse or domestic violence), along with most cases concerning education, employment, housing, welfare benefits, clinical negligence (with some exceptions) and other areas of law that impact on the lives of children and families. We can only guess at the potential impact of this legislation when it comes into force in April 2013. Resources within CAFCASS continue to be under strain and limitations remain on the availability of children's guardians in specified proceedings, with some child protection hearings taking place without the presence of a children's guardian. The LSC has also revised its franchise contracts with child and family lawyers, effectively reducing the funding currently available for child protection cases, and as a result, many of the experienced Children Panel practitioners have now abandoned that area of legal practice. For all the reasons outlined above, we continue to be greatly concerned about the welfare of children in need, and children who are at risk of significant harm. Our concern is shared by many of the judiciary, lawyers, children's guardians and social workers with whom we work.

We were pleased that the earlier editions of this book proved popular, and have maintained our aim to make this edition practical, easy to use and, above all, readable. 'He' and 'she' are used interchangeably in the text, for variety, and include either gender, where appropriate. This book provides brief notes on the salient points in child care and protection law and practice as it operates in England. Other jurisdictions, i.e. Scotland, Wales and Northern Ireland are covered where specifically mentioned. In a book intended to be concise and portable, it is always difficult to decide how much to include or omit, and we provide as many pointers as we can to additional cases, useful resources and reference works.

We feel that practice is enhanced by inter-disciplinary liaison and discussion between lawyers and practitioners from other disciplines working with children, sharing ideas and experience, debating thorny issues, tackling challenges and celebrating success.

We, too, welcome readers' ideas and feedback, and use information from practitioners to improve subsequent editions.

Despite all the current challenges, specialism in this area of law remains very rewarding, and necessary. We all feel that we are privileged to work with children and their families and with other practitioners actively involved in child care and protection.

Barbara Mitchels (Editor)

Acknowledgements

Many thanks to all those who have given their permission to include quotations, references and materials, and our particular appreciation to David Lane, formerly Senior Lecturer in Childhood Studies at Liverpool John Moores University, for his ideas, encouragement and helpful comments on the text.

We have also really appreciated the experience and help of Andrew Riddoch and Brian Hill from Wildy for their time and patience in working with us to design this fifth edition of the book.

Thank you, too, for the advice and help of the many professionals, volunteers, children and families over the years with whom each of us has worked. They often proved to be better sources of information and inspiration for improvement of practice than any law book could ever be.

Finally, our especial thanks to our own families, for their tolerance and patience while this was being written.

Barbara, Helen, Julie and Safda

Contents

1 Glossary and Legislative Framework

1.1 Glossary of basic definitions

Interpretations of many terms used within the Children Act 1989 are given in section 105. The source of definitions created by other sections, other Acts or by case law and other sources are cited. Unless otherwise stated, sections cited are from the Children Act 1989 (CA 1989).

Adoption agency

> Defined in section 2(1) of the Adoption and Children Act 2002 and includes local authorities and approved adoption organisations. Their work is regulated by the Adoption Agencies Regulations 2005, SI 2005/389 (as amended) and in Wales, the Adoption Agencies (Wales) Regulations 2005, SI 2005/1313.

Authorised person

> (a) In care and supervision proceedings, and in child assessment orders, this means the NSPCC or its officers, under sections 31(9) and 43(13) of the CA 1989. A person (other than a local authority) may be authorised by order of the Secretary of State to bring proceedings under section 31 for a care or supervision order, but no one has been so authorised.

> (b) In emergency protection orders, proceedings may be brought by an 'authorised officer' of the local authority, an 'authorised person' (as defined in (a) above), a 'designated' police officer or 'any other person'; see sections 31(9) and 44 of the CA 1989.

Authority

> The local authority of a geographical area, including county councils, district councils, unitary authorities in England and Wales, Welsh county councils and Welsh county borough councils.

Care order

> An order made under section 31(1)(a) of the CA 1989, placing a child in the care of a local authority. By section 31(11), this includes an interim care order made under section 38. By section 105, any reference to a child who is in the care of an authority is a reference to a child who is in the authority's care by virtue of a care order.

Child

> A person under the age of 18.

Child assessment order

> An order under section 43 of the CA 1989 to produce the child and to comply with the court's directions relating to the assessment of the child. There are restrictions on keeping the child away from home under this section.

Child in need

> Under section 17 of the CA 1989:
>
> > a child is taken to be in need if:
> >
> > (a) he is unlikely to achieve or maintain, or to have the opportunity of achieving or maintaining, a reasonable standard of health or development without the provision for him of services by a local authority;
> >
> > (b) his health or development is likely to be significantly impaired, or further impaired, without the provision for him of such services; or he is disabled.
>
> (Also, see *Assessing children in need and their families: Practice Guidance* (DoH, 2000) and *Framework for the assessment of children in need and their families* (DoH, 2000).)

Child looked after

> The term 'child looked after' is defined in section 22(1) of the CA 1989 and refers to a child who is subject to an interim care order made under section 38 or a full care order made under section 31(1)(a). It also includes a child who is accommodated by the local authority under section 20.

Child minder

> Defined in section 71 of the Care Standards Act 2000 as a person who looks after one or more children under the age of eight, for reward; for total period(s) exceeding two hours in any one day.

Child of the family

In relation to the parties to a marriage, under section 52 of the Matrimonial Causes Act 1973, this means: (a) a child of both of those parties; and (b) any other child, not being a child who is placed with those parties by a local authority or voluntary organisation, who has been treated by both of those parties as a child of their family.

Children and Family Court Advisory and Support Service

The Children and Family Court Advisory and Support Service (CAFCASS) is responsible for family court social work services in England. In Wales, this service is provided by CAFCASS Cymru.

Children's guardian

A social work practitioner appointed by the court to represent the child's interests in court proceedings. Children's guardians are provided by CAFCASS.

Children's home

Defined in section 1 of the Care Standards Act 2000 as a home which usually provides or is intended to provide care and accommodation wholly or mainly for children. Obviously, the section lists several exceptions, including the homes of parents, relatives, or those with parental responsibility for the children in question.

Community home

Defined in section 53 of the CA 1989 and may be: (a) a home provided, equipped and maintained by a local authority; or (b) provided by a voluntary organisation but in respect of which the management, equipment and maintenance of the home shall be the responsibility of the local authority or the responsibility of the voluntary organisation.

Contact order

Defined in section 8(1) of the CA 1989 as 'an order requiring the person with whom a child lives, or is to live, to allow the child to visit or stay with the person named in the order, or for that person and the child otherwise to have contact with each other'.

Contact with a child in care

Section 34 of the CA 1989 creates a presumption that a child subject to a care order will have contact with his or her parents, and contains provisions for determination of contact issues by the court.

Development

Defined in section 31(9) of the CA 1989 as physical, intellectual, emotional, social or behavioural development.

Disabled

Defined in section 17(11) of the CA 1989 and in relation to a child, means a child who is blind, deaf, or dumb or who suffers from mental disorder of any kind or who is substantially and permanently handicapped by illness, injury or congenital deformity or such other disability as may be prescribed.

Education supervision order

An order under section 36(1) of the CA 1989, putting the child with respect to whom the order is made under the supervision of a designated local education authority

Emergency protection order

Under section 44 of the CA 1989, this order is a direction for a child to be produced and authorises the local authority either to remove the child to a safe place or to stop the child from being removed by others from a hospital or other safe place.

Family assistance order

An order made under section 16 of the CA 1989 appointing a probation officer or an officer of the local authority to advise, assist and (where appropriate) befriend any person named in the order for a period of 12 months or less. Named persons may include parents, guardians, those with whom the child lives, or the child himself.

Family court adviser

A social work practitioner directed by the court to assist it by providing dispute resolution services in section 8 applications and/or reports under section 7 of the CA 1989.

Family proceedings

In the family proceedings court, all proceedings are treated as 'family proceedings' under section 92(2) of the CA 1989. However, in other courts, 'family proceedings' are defined in section 8(3) and (4) as including any proceedings:

(a)   under the inherent jurisdiction of the High Court in relation to children, including wardship but not applications for leave under section 100(3) of the CA 1989;

(b)   under Parts I, II and IV of the CA 1989; the Matrimonial Causes Act 1973; the Adoption and Children Act 2002; the Domestic Proceedings and Magistrates' Courts Act 1978; Part III of the Matrimonial and Family Proceedings Act 1984; the Family Law Act 1996; also under sections 11 and 12 of the Crime and Disorder Act 1998;

(c)   under section 30(8) of the Human Fertilisation and Embryology Act 1990, proceedings under section 30 of that Act are included.

(Note that the definitions in section 8(3) and (4) do not include applications for emergency protection orders, child assessment orders or recovery orders.)

Guardian

A guardian, appointed under section 5 of the CA 1989, for the child, but not for the child's estate. A guardian appointed under section 5 has parental responsibility for the child, following the death of one or both parents.

Harm

Defined in section 31(9) of the CA 1989, meaning the ill treatment or the impairment of health or development. Where the question of whether or not the harm is significant turns on the child's health and development, his health or development shall be compared with that which could be reasonably expected of a similar child, section 31(10).

Health

Under section 31 of the CA 1989, includes physical and mental health.

Hospital

Any health service hospital, and accommodation provided by the local authority and used as a hospital. It does not include special hospitals, which are those for people detained under the Mental Health Act 1983, providing secure hospital accommodation, section 105 of the CA 1989.

Ill treatment

Defined in section 31(9) of the CA 1989 and includes sexual abuse and forms of ill treatment which are not physical.

Independent reviewing officer

An independent reviewing officer (IRO) is appointed by the local authority to monitor the care planning process for looked after children. The IRO's functions are set out in *IRO Handbook: Statutory guidance for independent reviewing officers and local authorities on their functions in relation to case management and review for looked after children* (DfE, 2010).

Kinship care

Care for a child by family members or friends of the family. Kinship care may be arranged privately, on a voluntary basis, or as part of a care plan in the context of a care order.

Local authority

Under section 52 of the CA 1989, a council of a county, a metropolitan district, a London borough, or the Common Council of the City of London; in Scotland, it means a local authority under section 12 of the Social Work (Scotland) Act 1968.

Local authority foster carer

Defined in section 22(C)(12) of the CA 1989. A person with whom a child has been placed by a local authority under section 22. Local authority foster carers may include a family member; a relative of the child; or any other suitable person.

Local housing authority

Defined in the Housing Act 1944, meaning the district council, a London borough council, the Common Council of the City of London or Council of the Isles of Scilly.

Parent

The natural (birth) mother or father of a child, whether or not they are married to each other at the time of the birth or of conception. The CA 1989, when it states 'parent', means the birth parents of a child, including therefore natural fathers without parental responsibility. Where it intends to mean 'a parent with parental responsibility', it states so specifically.

Parent (in relation to adoption)

Under the Adoption and Children Act 2002, the consent of each 'parent or guardian of the child' must be obtained for adoption or dispensed with by the court. Section 52(6) of that Act defines 'parent' as 'a parent having parental responsibility for the child ...'. Once a child has been adopted, his or her birth parents are no longer legally 'parents' of the child. Former parents would therefore need leave to apply for section 8 orders after adoption if they wish to apply for contact after adoption.

Parent with parental responsibility

All mothers have parental responsibility for children born to them.

Fathers also have parental responsibility for their child if they married their child's mother before or after the child's birth. The father of a child who is not married to the mother is able to acquire parental responsibility in various ways under the CA 1989. This term therefore excludes the natural birth father of a child who has not acquired parental responsibility under the Act. See Chapter 3.

Parental responsibility

Defined in section 3 of the CA 1989 and includes all the rights, duties, powers, responsibilities and authority which by law a parent of a child has in relation to the child and his property. It can be acquired by unmarried fathers in respect of their child by registration of the birth with the mother after 1 December 2003, court order, or by a parental responsibility agreement under the CA 1989, and by others through residence or guardianship orders, or by a local authority under a care order. Parental responsibility can be shared with others. It ceases when the child reaches 18, on adoption, death, or cessation of the care order. See Chapter 3 for discussion.

Parental responsibility agreement

Defined in section 4(1) of the CA 1989 as an agreement between the father and mother of a child providing for the father to have parental responsibility for the child (a father married to the mother of their child at the time of the birth will automatically have parental responsibility for that child, but a father not so married will not). Format for the agreement is set out in the Parental Responsibility Agreement Regulations 1991, SI 1991/1478, as amended. See Chapter 3.

Private fostering

Defined in section 66 of the CA 1989. To 'foster a child privately' means looking after a child under the age of 16 (or, if disabled, 18), caring and providing accommodation for him or her, by someone who is not the child's parent, relative or who has parental responsibility for the child.

Prohibited steps order

Defined in section 8(1) of the CA 1989. An order that no step which could be taken by a parent in meeting his or her parental responsibility for a child, and which is of a kind specified in the order, shall be taken by any person without the consent of the court.

Public Law Outline

Referred to colloquially in court as 'the PLO', the *Public Law Outline* was issued as *Practice Direction: Guide to Case Management in Public Law Proceedings* by the President of the Family Division, and operative from 1 April 2008. It provides guidance on how family proceedings should be prepared, timetabled and presented in court, including expert evidence.

Relative

In relation to a child, this means a grandparent, brother, sister, uncle or aunt (whether of the full blood or of the half blood or by affinity) or step-parent, see section 105 of the CA 1989.

Residence order

An order under section 8(1) of the CA 1989 settling the arrangements to be made as to the person with whom a child is to live. This confers parental responsibility on the person who holds the order.

Responsible person

Defined in Schedule 3, paragraph 1 to the CA 1989. In relation to a supervised child, it means:

(a)   any person who has parental responsibility for the child; and

(b)   any other person with whom the child is living.

Service

In relation to any provision made under Part III of the CA 1989 (local authority support for children and families), this means any facility.

Special educational needs

These arise when there is a learning difficulty which calls for special educational provision to be made. These terms are defined in section 318 of the Education Act 1996.

Special guardian

A special guardianship order confers parental responsibility on the holder of the order, which she or he may exercise alone, excluding the parent. The provisions are found in sections 14A–F of the CA 1989.

Specific issue order

An order under section 8(1) of the CA 1989 giving directions for the purpose of determining a specific issue which has arisen, or which may arise, in connection with any aspect of parental responsibility for a child.

Supervision order

An order under section 31(1)(b) of the CA 1989 and (except where express provision to the contrary is made) includes an interim supervision order made under section 38.

Supervised child / supervisor

In relation to a supervision order or an education supervision order, these mean respectively the child who is (or is to be) under supervision and the person under whose supervision he is (or is to be) by virtue of the order.

Upbringing

In relation to any child, this includes the care of the child but not his maintenance.

Voluntary organisation

A body (other than a public or local authority) whose activities are not carried on for profit.

1.2 Orders available under the Children Act 1989

Order	Section	Maximum duration*
Parental responsibility	4	Age 18
Guardianship	5	Age 18
Residence	8	Age 18
Contact	8	Age 16 (18 in exceptional circumstances)
Prohibited steps	8	Age 16 (18 in exceptional circumstances)
Specific issue	8	Age 16 (18 in exceptional circumstances)
Special guardianship order	14A	Age 18 (or earlier revocation)
Family assistance order	16	12 months
Care order	31	Age 18
Interim care order	38	First, not more than eight weeks; remainder, maximum four weeks
Supervision order	31	Age 18; one year, may be extended to max total three years
Contact with a child in care	34	For duration of care order
Education supervision order	36	One year; repeatedly extensible for three years. Ceases at age 16
Child assessment	43	Seven days
Emergency protection	44	Eight days; extensible for further seven days

*   These orders may be brought to an end by court order, variation or discharge and subject to additional provisions. For details, please refer to the relevant chapter.

1.3 Introduction to the Children Act 1989

The Children Act 1989 (CA 1989) came into force on 19 October 1991, containing 108 sections and 15 Schedules, and was accompanied by the Family Proceedings Courts (Children Act 1989) Rules 1991, SI 1991/1395, the Family Proceedings (Children) Rules 1991, SI 1991/910 and several volumes of *The Children Act 1989 Guidance and Regulations* (DCSF) (*Guidance and Regulations*). The rules were replaced by the Family Procedure Rules 2010, SI 2010/2955 (FPR 2010) and most of the *Guidance and Regulations* have been gradually updated.

The CA 1989 created a new unified court system consisting of three tiers: the High Court, the county court and the family proceedings court (FPC), each of which has concurrent jurisdiction and powers. Appeals from the FPC lie to the county court or High Court and from the county court and High Court to the Court of Appeal and the Supreme Court. Cases may move up or down the tiers, transfers therefore being easier. The avoidance of delay is one of the underlying principles of the CA 1989. This Act, along with its subsidiary rules, created a new system of directions hearings to enable the courts to take firmer control of the timing of cases, admission of evidence and administrative matters.

The CA 1989 encourages families to stay together, imposing a duty on local authorities to provide services for children in need and their families, to reduce the necessity for children to be looked after away from home, and for child protection proceedings. Unless the criteria for the making of care or supervision orders are met, an order cannot be made. The courts, if concerned about the welfare of a child, may order a local authority to investigate the child's circumstances, but the courts have no power of their own volition to order a child into the care of a local authority.

The CA 1989 introduced a new concept of parental responsibility, which unmarried fathers may gain in relation to their children, and which is accessible to other adults, such as grandparents or step-parents, who may apply for residence orders or special guardianship. It also creates orders governing aspects of a child's life, that is, contact with others, residence and resolution of disputed aspects of child care – prohibited steps (forbidding actions) and specific issues (permitting actions to take place).

The principles behind the CA 1989 and its guidance are that children are people whose rights are to be respected, not just 'objects of concern', and that children should wherever possible remain with their families, helped if necessary by provision of services, provided that their welfare is safeguarded. An atmosphere of negotiation and co-operation between professionals is encouraged. The welfare of the child is paramount, and, in the field of child care and protection, professionals are expected to work together in a non-adversarial way for the benefit of the child.

Section 6 of the Human Rights Act 1998 makes it unlawful for public authorities to act in ways incompatible with the rights set out in the European Convention for the Protection of Human Rights and Fundamental Freedoms 1950 (ECHR). This includes courts, tribunals and local authorities, including both acts and omissions (section 6). Those affected may bring proceedings or rely on the ECHR (section 7) by way of an appeal, complaint or judicial review.

1.4   Introduction to *Every Child Matters* and the Children Act 2004

Every Child Matters: Change for Children, a green paper setting out the government's vision for children's services, was published in September 2003, and the recommended changes are now being implemented through the Children Act 2004.

There are differences between England and Wales in the way the 2004 Act is implemented. A guide to child law in Wales is available at www.ccwales.org.uk/child-law/.

In Scotland, *It's Everyone's Job to Make Sure that I'm Alright*, the report of the Child Protection Audit Review carried out across Scotland, was published in November 2002, and a programme of reforms are now being implemented, see for example the Commissioner for Children and Young People (Scotland) Act 2003, *Protecting Children and Young People: The Charter* (Scottish Executive, 2004) and *Protecting Children and Young People: The Framework for Standards* (Scottish Executive, 2004).

The Children Act 2004 creates a structure of duties and responsibility shared between national government, local government and non-governmental organisations to provide 'children's services'. For further details of the provisions for implementation, see the Children Act 2004 (Children's Services) Regulations 2005, SI 2005/1972.

Under these provisions, local authorities are empowered to set up arrangements for co-operation among local partners: district councils, police, probation service, youth offending teams, strategic health authorities, primary care trusts, Connexions and the Learning and Skills Council. These are all implemented through the Children's Trust, with participation by schools, GP practices, culture, sports and play organisations and the voluntary and community sector.

These organisations should have clear policies and procedures for co-operation in child protection, including procedures for information sharing for the benefit of the child or young person.

The CA 1989 places a statutory duty on health, education and other services to help the local authority in carrying out its functions under the Act (similar provisions exist in the Children (Scotland) Act 1995 and *Protecting Children – A shared responsibility – Guidance on Inter-Agency Co-operation* (Scottish Office, 1998). There is a statutory duty to work together, including information sharing, in conducting initial investigations of children who may be in need or subject to abuse and in the more detailed core assessments carried out under section 47 of the CA 1989. For details of the assessment process, see also *Framework for the assessment of children in need and their families* (DoH, 2000).

Working Together to Safeguard Children: A guide to inter-agency working to safeguard and promote the welfare of children (DCSF, 2010), and its supporting materials, are all available from the website, www.education.gov.uk. Other useful references are *Information Sharing – A Practitioner's Guide* (DfES, 2006), *What to Do if You're Worried a Child is being Abused* (DfES, 2006) and *Confidentiality: NHS Code of Practice* (DoH, 2003).

2 Principles Underlying the Children Act 1989

2.1 Paramountcy of the welfare of the child

The Children Act 1989 (CA 1989) commences with a clear direction in section 1(1) that:

> When a court determines any question with respect to—
>
> (a) the upbringing of a child; or
>
> (b) the administration of a child's property or the application of any income arising from it,
>
> the child's welfare shall be the paramount consideration.

This means that after weighing all the factors, the court's decision will be made in accordance with the child's welfare. The child's welfare is not paramount if the decision is not about his or her upbringing or is not one being made within court proceedings.

The child's welfare is not always easy to determine, and so the CA 1989 sets out a list of criteria in section 1(3), known as the 'welfare checklist'. It is primarily intended as an aide-memoire, particularly useful for judges, children's guardians, professional and expert witnesses, but the court must have regard to it when considering an application to vary or discharge an order under Part IV (a child protection order), a special guardianship order, or a contested section 8 order for contact, residence, specific issue or prohibited steps, and magistrates should always refer to the checklist when considering their findings of fact and reasons for their decisions.

The welfare checklist is not compulsory in other circumstances, but it is always useful for practitioners to consider it. If experts refer to these criteria whilst writing their reports, they will ensure that they are complying with the principles of the CA 1989.

2.1.1 Welfare checklist

(a) The ascertainable wishes and feelings of the child concerned (considered in the light of his age and understanding).

(b)   His physical, emotional and educational needs.

(c)   The likely effect on him of any change in his circumstances.

(d)   His age, sex, background and any characteristics of his which the court considers relevant.

(e)   Any harm which he is suffering or which he is at risk of suffering.

(f)   How capable each of his parents, and any other person in relation to whom the court considers the question to be relevant, is of meeting his needs.

(g)   The range of powers available to the court under this Act in the proceedings in question.

In private law cases (those between individuals as opposed to those involving state intervention in a family's life), in proceedings that are not 'specified proceedings' listed in section 41 of the CA 1989, the court may ask the family court adviser to investigate the child's circumstances and to report back to the court the child's wishes and feelings, also advising the court on the best way to safeguard the child's welfare.

The court should be alert to any unusual circumstances or factors of concern in private law cases, even if the parties themselves are in agreement. The court may, where there is a concern, make a direction to the local authority to investigate the child's circumstances under section 37 of the CA 1989 and appoint a children's guardian to safeguard the welfare of the child at the same time.

The court may also make orders under section 8 or section 16 of the CA 1989 (family assistance) orders of its own volition, if necessary.

Where there is more than one child subject to an application, the court must consider the welfare of each and try to achieve the right balance. However, in *Birmingham CC v H* [1994] 1 All ER 12, [1994] 1 FLR 224, the court held that in a Part IV application concerning a child whose parent was herself still a minor, only the welfare of the child subject to the application was paramount.

2.2   Delay is deemed prejudicial to child's interests (the impact of the *Public Law Outline*)

In proceedings in which any question with respect to the upbringing of a child arises, the court shall have regard to the general principle that any delay in determining the question is likely to prejudice the welfare of the child, section 1(2) of the CA 1989.

The courts have been greatly concerned about delays in the family court system. One attempt at grasping the nettle was an interim *Protocol for Judicial Case Management* issued in 2003. This has been replaced by the *Public Law Outline* (PLO), issued as *Practice Direction: Guide to Case Management in Public Law Proceedings* by the President of the Family Division, and operative from 1 April 2008. The Direction was revised in April 2010 (*Practice Direction: Public Law Proceedings Guide to Case Management*, April 2010) and is available on the Judiciary of England and Wales website, www.judiciary.gov.uk.

Under the PLO, the cases progress through four stages:

(1) pre-proceedings up until the end of the first appointment in court;

(2) the advocates meeting and the case management stage;

(3) issues resolution hearing and the preceding advocates meeting;

(4) final hearing and directions for disclosure at the conclusion of the case.

The court regulates the conduct of cases by use of questionnaires, pro formas, meetings, hearings and directions. In these, the court establishes who are parties to, or who should have notice of, the proceedings. The court ensures that the evidence is in order and service is carried out. A timetable is set for preparation of the case and disclosure of evidence to other parties and the children's guardian, and a hearing date is fixed. Directions given carry the force of court orders, failure to comply with them will be viewed by the court seriously and a full explanation for non-compliance will be required. Sanctions include wasted costs orders against those parties to a case who cause (or negligently allow) unnecessary delay. For the Court of Appeal's guidance on wasted costs, see *Ridelhalgh v Horsfield and Watson v Watson* [1994] 3 WLR 462, [1994] 2 FLR 194.

A recommendation from the recent *Family Justice Review* (*Family Justice Review Final Report* (Ministry of Justice, 2011)) is that care proceedings under section 31 of the CA 1989 should have a time limit imposed of six months. Although this recommendation has been accepted by the government, it is thought that such a change would require primary legislation. Pending any such amendment, HM Courts & Tribunals Service is piloting a case management system in 2012–13 which is intended to track reasons for any delay in care cases which are not completed within a 26-week 'pathway'.

2.3 No order unless necessary in the interests of the child

The CA 1989 assumes that the parties will do their best to resolve differences by negotiation and co-operation. Section 1(5) provides that the court has a positive duty not to make an order unless it is in the interests of the child to do so. This is referred to as the 'non-intervention' principle and applies primarily to applications in private law disputes where agreement may have been reached.

However, the Court of Appeal held in *Re G (Children) (Residence: Making of Order)* [2005] EWCA Civ 1283 that section 1(5) of the CA 1989 does not create any presumption against making an order, just that the court will ask whether it will be better for the child to make an order than not to make one.

3 Parental Responsibility

On 19 October 1991, sections 2 and 3 of the Children Act 1989 (CA 1989) changed the status of parents in relation to their children, by creating the concept of 'parental responsibility'.

Amazingly, many parents are still unaware of these changes, and they are also unaware that not all parents will have parental responsibility for their children. Parental responsibility may be shared with others and it may be delegated in part, but it may not be surrendered or transferred entirely, save by adoption. Each person who has parental responsibility may exercise it without a duty to consult others who also have it, with certain exceptions, but in the event of disagreement or a need for child protection, its exercise is also subject to orders of the court. People who have a special guardianship order in their favour may exercise their parental responsibility in priority over others.

3.1 Definition, powers and duties of parental responsibility

Section 3(1) of the CA 1989 defines parental responsibility as, 'All the rights, duties, powers, responsibilities and authority which by law a parent of a child has in relation to the child and his property'.

This wonderfully vague definition is not clarified anywhere in the CA 1989 except in section 3(2), which states that parental responsibility includes the powers of a guardian in looking after a child's property, for example, to give a valid receipt for a legacy. *Introduction to the Children Act 1989* (DCSF 1991), paragraph 1.4 says: 'That choice of words emphasises that the duty to care for the child and to raise him to moral, physical, and emotional health is the fundamental task of parenthood and the only justification for the authority it confers'.

The Children Act 1989 Guidance and Regulations (DCSF), Volume 1 *Court Orders*, paragraph 2.6, says that parental responsibility is concerned with bringing the child up, caring for him and making decisions about him, but does not affect the relationship of parent and child for other purposes. It does not affect rights of maintenance or succession.

Some statutory powers are reliant upon parental responsibility:

(a)   appointment of guardian for a child in the event of death, section 5(3) of the CA 1989;

(b)   consent to the adoption of the child, section 19(1) and (2) of the Adoption and Children Act 2002; parent in this context is defined as a 'parent' with parental responsibility under section 52(5);

(c)   access to the child's medical records, sections 4, 5 and 12 of the Access to Health Records Act 1990;

(d)   consent to a child's marriage, section 1 of the Marriage Act 1941, as amended by Schedule 12, paragraph 5 to the CA 1989;

(e)   consent of all those with parental responsibility or leave of the court is required for removal of a child from the country, failing which a criminal offence is committed, section 1 of the Child Abduction and Custody Act 1985.

This provision applies even if there is a residence order in force, but under section 13(2) of the CA 1989, the person holding a residence order in his or her favour may take the child abroad for holiday purposes for up to one month. The court may, of course, grant additional or general leave to take the child abroad for longer periods or permanently.

Other decisions and powers of those with parental responsibility include:

(a)   Consent to medical assessment, examination or treatment. See para 3.1.2 and Chapter 12. 'Nearest relative' in section 27(2) of the Mental Health Act 1983 is now amended to substitute for the word 'mother' both the mother and the father who has parental responsibility within the meaning of section 3 of the CA 1989.

(b)   Lawful correction. It is a defence to assault or to a charge of ill treating a child under section 1 of the Children and Young Persons Act 1933 for a parent to prove that the act was one of 'lawful correction'. The correction must be 'moderate in manner, instrument and quantity'. See *R v H (Assault of Child: Reasonable Chastisement)* [2001] EWCA Crim 1024, [2001] 2 FLR 431.

(c)   Application for or veto of child's passport. See *Practice Direction (Disclosure of Addresses)* [1986] 1 All ER 977 at 981 and *Re A* [1995] 1 FLR 767. Also note PD 12P accompanying the FPR 2010, which sets out the situations surrounding the removal from the jurisdiction, and the issue of passports for children who are a ward of court.

(d)   Right to represent child as 'litigation friend' in all court proceedings where the child is a party, except cases involving child protection or the upbringing of the child. The right can be removed if the parents act improperly or against the interests of the child (Order 80, rule 2 of the Rules of the Supreme Court 1965, SI 1965/1776; Order 10, rule 1 of the County Court Rules 1981, SI 1981/1687).

Note that for those cases where the child is a party in children cases, they are classed as 'protected parties' under Part 15 of the FPR 2010. Part 15 provides for the appointment of a litigation friend to conduct proceedings on behalf of the protected party. The terms 'next friend' and 'guardian ad litem' are removed. Part 16 contains provisions for the representation of children in 'specified' proceedings, as well as other proceedings, including, in particular, adoption proceedings.

(e)   Right to name or re-name child. If both parents have parental responsibility and they agree, there is no problem. Note *Practice Direction* [1995] 1 FLR 458 and *Re PC (Change of Surname)* [1997] 2 FLR 730 for guidance. In cases where one parent wishes to change a child's name, the consent of all others with parental responsibility – or in the absence of consent, the leave of the court – is required. See, also, the Enrolment of Deeds (Change of Name) (Amendment) Regulations 2005, SI 2005/2056 and the Enrolment of Deeds (Change of Name) Regulations 1994, SI 1994/604 (reproduced in the Appendix to PD 5A accompanying the FPR 2010.

(f)   Registration of child's name. Under the Births and Deaths Registration Act 1953, a baby's name must be registered within 42 days of birth. Parents with parental responsibility may register the name. Fathers without parental responsibility, therefore, have no power to choose or register the baby's name without an order of the court. See *Re PK, Re A and Re B (Change of Name)* [1999] 2 FLR 930 and the House of Lords in *Dawson v Wearmouth* [1999] 2 WLR 960, [1999] 1 FLR 1167. Note, however, joint registration of birth at para 3.4.3. Also consider the case of *F v F* [2007] EWHC 2543 (Fam), [2008] 1 FLR 1163, which considers the situations where a change of surname may be warranted, in order to generate improvement in the child's welfare.

(g)   Right to decide child's education and duty to send child to school, or to provide suitable alternative schooling (Education Acts 1962 and 1944). Section 7 of the Education Act 1996 requires the parent of a child of compulsory schooling age to ensure that the child receives full-time education, suitable to his or her age, ability and aptitude, and to any special education needs the child may have. Schedule 13, paragraph 10 to the CA 1989 includes those who are not parents but who have parental responsibility for the child. See *Re Z (Minor) (Freedom of Publication)* [1996] 2 WLR 107, [1996] 1 FLR 191 on education, medical consent and publication of information.

(h) Decisions about a child's religion. The courts will not interfere unless the welfare of the child is threatened. Consider also, for example, sensitive cases involving circumcision, such as *Re S (Specific Issue Order: Religion: Circumcision)* [2004] EWHC 1282 (Fam), [2005] 1 FLR 236. In this case, the court decided that children of dual religious heritage should be entitled to practice both faiths in appropriate cases, and that they should be allowed to decide for themselves which, if any, religion they sought to follow. Also, see the more recent case of *Re N (A Child: Religion – Jehovah's Witness)* [2011] EWHC B26 (Fam), where the court stressed that parental responsibility is joint and equal, and that one parent does not have a right to unilaterally determine the child's religion.

3.1.1 Duration

Parental responsibility lasts until a child is 18 years old if it belongs to the mother, to the child's married father, to the father with a parental responsibility agreement, legitimation or joint registration, or to any other person with a court order. Parental responsibility can be ordered with residence orders or guardianship. See paras 3.4.4. and 3.5.4.

3.1.2 Parental responsibility and medical consent

Save in emergencies, no person may be given medical treatment without consent. Whatever the motivation, this may constitute an assault for which practitioners may incur liability in tort or criminal law. Detention in hospital or any other place without consent could constitute false imprisonment. Those with parental responsibility, or a court, may give consent for medical assessment or treatment of a child. In emergencies, where there is no person capable or available to give or withhold consent, the doctor may lawfully treat the patient.

Medical records should note who has parental responsibility for a child. With unmarried parents, in the absence of a parental responsibility agreement, joint registration or court order, only the mother will have parental responsibility for the child. Should she (or any lone person with parental responsibility) die there will be no one with parental responsibility for the child. Single parents should therefore appoint a guardian for their child; see para 3.5.4.

Young people aged 16 and over

Section 8 of the Family Law Reform Act 1969 confers on a person of 16 the right to give informed consent to surgical, medical or dental treatment. Examinations or assessments could also impliedly be included. Those who suffer mental illness, disability or psychiatric disturbance will be subject to the same mental health provisions and safeguards as adults.

Children aged under 16

See Chapter 12, paras 12.1 and 12.2.

In *Gillick v West Norfolk and Wisbech AHA* [1986] AC 112, Mrs Gillick challenged her local health authority's provision of contraceptive advice to her daughters under 16 without her consent. The House of Lords supported the health authority's actions. In giving judgment, it formulated the concept known colloquially as '*Gillick* competence'. A child under 16 may make medical decisions according to her chronological age, in conjunction with mental and emotional maturity, intelligence, her comprehension of the nature and consequences of the decision to be made and the quality of the information provided.

The rationale of the *Gillick* case has been considered and approved in *R (Axon) v Secretary of State for Health* [2006] EWHC 37 (Admin) QBD, in which abortion for a child under 16 was the subject of the court's consideration. Although distinctions could be made between the issues in *Gillick*, i.e. advice and treatment for contraception and sexually transmitted illnesses on the one hand and abortion in the *Axon* case on the other, which gave rise to more serious and complex issues, the guidelines set out in *Gillick*, properly adapted, were considered appropriate as guidance in respect of all sexual matters. That was because the majority in *Gillick* did not indicate that their conclusions were dependent on the nature of the treatment proposed. The *Gillick* guidelines are of general application to all forms of medial advice and treatment.

In the case of *Re R (Minor: Consent to Medical Treatment)* [1992] Fam 11, [1992] 1 FLR 190, the Court of Appeal held that a '*Gillick*-competent' child acquires a right to make decisions equal to that of each of his parents and only the absence of consent by all having that power would create a veto. If they cannot agree, then the doctor lawfully may act on consent of one. However, *A Guide to Consent for Examination or Treatment*, produced by the National Health Service Management Executive, advises that the refusal of an adult or '*Gillick*-competent' young person should be respected.

In this context, paragraph 79 of *Consent guidance: patients and doctors making decisions together* (General Medical Council, 2008), provides that when an emergency arises in a clinical setting and it is not possible to find out a patient's wishes, a doctor can treat the patient without his or her consent, provided the treatment is immediately necessary to save the patient's life or to prevent a serious deterioration of his or her condition. The treatment must be the least restrictive of the patient's future choices.

In relation to medical examination of children, *The Physical Signs of Child Sexual Abuse: An evidence-based review and guidance for best practice* (RCPCH, 2008) relates to the physical signs of child sexual abuse. This publication is produced by the Royal College of Paediatrics and Child Health, in collaboration with the Royal College of Physicians of London and its Faculty of Forensic and Legal Medicine.

If there is disagreement or refusal concerning medical treatment for a child when a doctor considers it medically necessary, and negotiation fails, then the matter can be resolved under section 8 of the CA 1989 by a specific issue order. The High Court in its inherent jurisdiction or under the CA 1989 can override the wishes of anyone in relation to the medical treatment of a child if this is adjudged to be in the child's best interests.

3.1.3 What if there is no one with parental responsibility?

Where immediate action is needed for the welfare of the child and no one with parental responsibility is available, section 3(5) of the CA 1989 provides that:

A person who:

(a) does not have parental responsibility for a particular child; but

(b) has care of the child, may ... do what is reasonable in all the circumstances of the case for the purpose of safeguarding or promoting the child's welfare.

This could apply to childminders, foster carers, neighbours and others looking after children who may need to take a child quickly to the GP or dentist, etc. This section, however, is not intended to cover consent for major medical issues.

3.2 Legal position of child's birth mother

Parental responsibility always belongs to a mother in relation to the children to whom she has given birth. It does not matter whether or not she is married to the father of the child (or to anyone else). Nothing can remove that parental responsibility from her save death or adoption of the child. For surrogacy arrangements, see paras 3.5.6 and 3.5.7.

3.3 Legal position of child's father

3.3.1 Married fathers

Under section 2(1) of the CA 1989, a father automatically has parental responsibility for his child if he was married to the child's mother at the time of the child's birth. This concept includes marriage at the time of the child's conception. See *Re Overbury (Deceased)* [1954] 3 All ER 308. The man must be the biological father. Section 1(2)–(4) of the Family Law Reform Act 1987 includes in the meaning of section 2(1) children who are legitimated by statute. This enables a child's father to gain parental responsibility if he subsequently marries the child's mother after conception or the birth of the child.

We are told by clients that many married couple's arguments have ended with '… and anyway she is not your child!'. The parents of a legitimate child have parental responsibility for that child. The test of legitimacy is that the child is born to parents who are married to each other at the time of the child's birth. Section 1(2) and (3) of the Family Law Reform Act 1987 includes children who are legitimated by their parents' subsequent marriage. A child's legitimacy may be rebutted by cogent evidence, for example, a DNA paternity test showing that the husband is not the father of the child. A married man has no parental responsibility for children who are not biologically his own, even if they are born during the marriage.

Children born to a married couple as a result of artificial insemination will, however, be regarded as the child of the husband provided that the conditions set out in the Human Fertilisation and Embryology Act 2008 (HFEA 2008) are met.

Note that men who become step-parents on marriage do not automatically acquire parental responsibility for their spouses' children, see para 3.5.2.

3.3.2 Unmarried fathers

A father who is not married to the mother of his child has no parental responsibility, but he can acquire it in a number of ways. These are set out below.

3.4 Acquisition and loss of parental responsibility by child's birth father

3.4.1 Parental responsibility order

A father may apply under section 4(1)(a) of the CA 1989 for a parental responsibility order.

Applicant

> The father without parental responsibility, section 4(1) of the CA 1989. Also, the spouse or civil partner who has parental responsibility for the child (section 4A), as well as the second female legal parent pursuant to section 43 of the HFEA 2008 (no one else can apply).

Attendance

> All parties shall attend, unless otherwise directed, rule 12.14(3) of the FPR 2010. The rules make an exception that proceedings shall take place in the absence of any party (including the child) if he is represented by children's guardian or solicitor, and it is in the child's interests having regard to the issues or evidence, rule 12.14(3).

Issues for the court

> Degree of attachment between father and child; commitment shown by father to child; the reasons for the application (not improper or wrong). CA 1989 principles – welfare of child paramount, no delay and no order unless it is in best interests of child to make it.
>
> Relevant cases: *Re G (Minor) (Parental Responsibility Order)* [1994] 1 FLR 504, *Re T (Minor) (Parental Responsibility)* [1993] 2 FLR 450, *Re S (Parental Responsibility)* [1995] 2 FLR 648, *Re M (Contact: Family Assistance: McKenzie Friend)* [1999] 1 FLR 75 and *Re J (Parental Responsibility)* [1999] 1 FLR 784.
>
> Also, see more recent case law, which has considered the concept of 'parenthood' in disputes surrounding parental responsibility. In particular, consider *Re D (Contact and PR: Lesbian Mothers and Known*

Father) (No 2) [2006] EWHC 2 (Fam), [2006] 1 FCR 556 whereby Black J made use of 'recitals' in applications for parental responsibility by the father. Contrast this case, however, with the case of *R v E and F (Female Parents: Known Father)* [2010] EWHC 417 (Fam), [2010] 2 FLR 383, whereby Bennett J decided that the father of the child had a key role to play in the child's life, but was not on an 'equal footing' with the mother and her partner.

Notice

Local authority providing accommodation for the child. Also, person(s) with whom the child is living at time of application, and those providing a refuge need to be served with form C6A, PD 12C, paragraph 3.1 accompanying the FPR 2010.

Parties / respondents

All those with parental responsibility (or if a care order is in force, those who had parental responsibility immediately prior to that order), rule 12.3 of the FPR 2010.

On discharge application, all parties to the original proceedings will be respondents, as well as the respondent to the parental responsibility application, rule 12.3 of the FPR 2010.

Procedural notes

Family proceedings under the CA 1989. Application on form C1. Also, form FM1 is to be sent to court (pursuant to PD 3A accompanying the FPR 2010). Form C1A is also to be sent to court if it is alleged that the child, who is the subject to the application, has suffered, or is at risk of suffering significant harm, in the form of domestic abuse, violence, abduction, or other behaviour.

Service at least 14 days before date of directions/hearing, PD 12C accompanying the FPR 2010. Respondents are served with notice in form C6, and the application, PD 12C, paragraph 3.1 accompanying the FPR 2010. Individuals can be joined to the application for parental responsibility by applying in form C2, rule 12.3(3) of the FPR 2010. The court can also join people using their general case management powers in making the order for joinder of its own initiative, pursuant to rule 4.3. The remaining procedure is the same as for section 8 applications, see Chapter 13; see in particular the Private Law Programme, now contained as PD 12B accompanying the FPR 2010.

Status of child

> With leave, a child of sufficient age and understanding can oppose the application or apply to set aside the order.

3.4.2   Parental responsibility agreement with the mother

The mother and father may agree that the father shall have parental responsibility for the child. The agreement must be made in accordance with the Children (Parental Responsibility Agreement) Regulations 1991, SI 1991/1478 as amended by the Parental Responsibility Agreement (Amendment) Regulations 1994, SI 1994/3157, the Parental Responsibility Agreement (Amendment) Regulations 2005, SI 2005/2808 and the Parental Responsibility Agreement (Amendment) Regulations 2009, SI 2009/2026. Note that the latter statutory instrument amends the previous regulations, so as to provide for the acquisition of parental responsibility by a second female parent. This involves completion of form C (PRA3), as from September 2009.

The prescribed form C (PRA1) for use by the mother of the child and the father is straightforward and must be completed, signed by the mother and father and witnessed by a Justice of the Peace, justices' clerk or a court officer. The child's birth certificate should be produced, together with proof of identity incorporating a signature and photograph, for example a photocard driving licence, official pass or passport.

Note that, under section 4A of the CA 1989, a step-parent who is the married partner or (following the implementation of the Civil Partnership Act 2004) who is the civil partner of a parent with parental responsibility for a child may enter into a parental responsibility agreement with the parent(s) of the child. In this case, the parental responsibility agreement will be on form C (PRA2) and the same proofs of identity will be required. In addition, proof of the marriage or civil registration will be necessary. The completed and witnessed form C (PRA2) then has to be registered with the Principal Registry of the Family Division, at First Avenue House, 42–49 High Holborn, London, WC1V 6NP, and will take effect once it is registered. A copy is sent to each parent. Form C (PRA3), referred to above, for the second female legal parent, must also be completed.

Precedents for all three forms are set out in the Schedule to the Parental Responsibility Agreement (Amendment) Regulations 2009, SI 2009/2026. They are available online at www.legislation.gov.uk.

3.4.3 Joint registration of the birth by father and mother

This was a new provision brought in by the Adoption and Children Act 2002 and it applies only to registrations of birth made on or after 1 December 2003. It is possible to re-register the birth of a child born before this date, where the original registration did not name the father, provided that the requirements of section 10(a) of the Births and Deaths registration Act 1953 are met. In these circumstances, the parental responsibility will run from the date of registration and not from the date of birth. The mother must agree to the inclusion of the father at the registration of the birth. Registration can unilaterally be applied for where there is a court order in force for parental responsibility or financial relief, or a parental responsibility agreement is in force.

3.4.4 Residence order and parental responsibility

A child's father may acquire a residence order under section 8 of the CA 1989. This may be granted on application or of the court's own initiative in the course of family proceedings, see Chapter 13.

The court has power to award parental responsibility with residence orders which subsists while the order remains in force. Pursuant to section 37 of the Children and Young Persons Act 2008, section 8 of the CA 1989 is amended, with the effect that as from September 2009, the age at which a residence order automatically ends is raised from 16 to 18 years of age, unless the court decides otherwise.

There are special provisions in the CA 1989 when the father of a child acquires a residence order relating to his child. On making the residence order, the court must also grant parental responsibility to the father, under sections 4 and 12(1) of the CA 1989. The court shall not bring that parental responsibility order to an end whilst the residence order remains in force. The parental responsibility so granted will not expire if the residence order is revoked, but will last until the child is 18, unless the court specifically brings the father's parental responsibility to an end earlier, section 91(7).

In specific circumstances, the father of a child who does not have parental responsibility may also acquire it (in the same way as another relative or non-relative might), through one or more of the ways outlined in para 3.5, where an application is open to him, for example, where appropriate, he may apply for guardianship.

3.5   Acquisition of parental responsibility by others

3.5.1   Relatives

Relatives can obtain parental responsibility for a child along with a residence order under sections 8 and 12(2) of the CA 1989. Relatives could also seek an appointment under section 5 as guardian of the child, which automatically gives them parental responsibility until the child reaches 18 or the court orders otherwise, section 91(7).

A relative could also, in theory, apply to adopt a child in order to gain parental responsibility. Courts will not usually favour adoption by relatives because the effect of adoption is to sever all legal ties with existing parents and therefore may complicate family relationships, but in specific circumstances it may be considered appropriate.

In referring to relatives, it is important to note that, in relation to applications under the CA 1989, civil partners are treated in law in the same way as a married spouse. For example, a civil partner of a parent with parental responsibility can enter into a parental responsibility agreement with that child's parent(s), subject to certain conditions, see para 3.4.

3.5.2   Step-parents

Step-parents do not acquire parental responsibility for the children of their partners automatically on marriage. Currently, they can only acquire parental responsibility along with a residence order under sections 8 and 12(2) of the CA 1989, or by adoption.

The courts would not normally favour adoption by a step-father unless the natural father is deceased, whether or not the natural father had parental responsibility, since adoption would sever his legal responsibility for, and relationship with, his child.

A step-parent who is married to a parent with parental responsibility of the child or who is the civil partner of that parent, can acquire parental responsibility for the child by entering into a parental responsibility agreement with the parent(s) of the child under section 4 of the CA 1989. For details of how to do this, see para 3.4.2.

The mother of a child (who always has parental responsibility herself) may develop terminal illness or die whilst in a relationship with a man who is not the father of her child. The child may be very attached to him and he may be committed to the care of the child.

If the child's mother dies, there are three possible scenarios:

(a)   *The child's biological father is alive but has no parental responsibility. The child will then legally have no one with parental responsibility.*

Remedies:

- before the mother's death, the stepfather obtains a residence order alone or shared with the mother;

- mother appoints the stepfather guardian under section 5 of the CA 1989;

- if the mother has died, the stepfather may obtain a residence order or guardianship order under section 5(1)(a). Guardianship automatically gives him parental responsibility until the child reaches 18 or the court orders otherwise, section 91(7).

The step-parent may apply for a special guardianship order under section 14A of the CA 1989 which will enable him to have parental responsibility for the child and create stronger legal ties with the child, but this is less final than adoption, which would sever legal links with the child's birth family. Under a special guardianship order, links with the child's birth family are retained.

(b)   *The child's biological father is alive and has parental responsibility.*

The biological father will then automatically hold the legal responsibility for the child.

The stepfather can seek a residence order. If he has been appointed as guardian by the mother before her death, this will only be effective immediately if she had a residence order in her favour before her death, section 5(7)(b) of the CA 1989. He could seek guardianship under section 5(1)(b) if the deceased mother had a residence order in her favour. In either case, he would have to share parental responsibility with the biological father and resolve disputes by seeking an appropriate section 8 order. See Chapter 13 for discussion of section 8 orders.

The stepfather can enter into a parental responsibility agreement with the father who has parental responsibility, under section 4 of the CA 1989 (see para 3.4.2).

(c)   *The biological father is dead, therefore there is no one with parental responsibility for this child.*

The stepfather can seek a residence order under section 8 or guardianship under section 5(1)(a) of the CA 1989. Guardianship automatically gives him parental responsibility until the child reaches 18 or the court orders otherwise, section 91(7).

The stepmother of a child, living with the child's father, would face similar problems on his death. The child's mother would always have parental responsibility. She would have a legal right to the care of the child unless otherwise agreed or ordered by the court. The stepmother could seek a residence order or guardianship, if the father had a residence order in force in his favour at the time of his death.

3.5.3 Non-relatives

Non-relatives may acquire parental responsibility with a residence order or through guardianship, special guardianship or adoption.

A local authority obtains parental responsibility for a child under section 31 of the CA 1989 when a care order is made, sharing parental responsibility with the child's mother and anyone else who has it. The exercise by others of their parental responsibility in relation to the child may be limited by the local authority under the care order, but there should be partnership and co-operation. The local authority does not acquire parental responsibility when looking after children in voluntary arrangements.

3.5.4 Guardianship

The court may appoint a guardian for a child under section 5 of the CA 1989 where:

- there is no person with parental responsibility for the child; or

- a residence order has been made in favour of a parent or guardian who died whilst the order was in force.

This parental responsibility subsists until the child reaches 18, unless ended earlier by the court, section 91(7).

A parent with parental responsibility, or a guardian, may appoint a guardian for a child in the event of his death under section 5(3) and (4) of the CA 1989 respectively. If when he dies there is no one else alive with parental responsibility, the appointed guardian will act. If there is anyone with parental responsibility still alive, then the guardian will only be able to act after the death of all others with parental responsibility. If, however, someone with a residence order in her favour appoints a guardian, she will act on the death of the appointer, in conjunction with anyone else remaining alive who has parental responsibility

3.5.5 Special guardianship order

Special guardianship is an order created by the Adoption and Children Act 2002 and imported into the CA 1989 as section 14A. The court can make this order in public or private law proceedings and under the Adoption and Children Act 2002.

The effects of a special guardianship order are that:

- the special guardian has parental responsibility for the child until the child reaches 18;

- special guardians can exercise their parental responsibility to the exclusion of others who have it (other than another special guardian, section 14(1)(b) of the CA 1989);

- the child's parents are specifically excluded from application.

The persons who can apply are set out in section 14A(5)(a)–(e) of the CA 1989. They include (in relation to that child):

- any guardian;

- people with a residence order in their favour;

- anyone listed under section 10(5)(b) and (c);

- a relative (defined under section 105(1)) with whom the child has lived for a period of at least one year immediately before they make the application (section 14(5)(e)). This provision came into effect as a result of section 38 of the Children and Young Persons Act 2008, in September 2009;

- a local authority foster carer with whom the child has lived for at least one year immediately before he or she applies;

- any person with permission of the court, section 10(8) and (9) of the CA 1989.

Therefore, it includes under section 10(5)(b) and (c) of the CA 1989 the following list of people:

(a) any person with whom the child has lived for a period of at least three years;

(b) any person who—

(i) in any case where a residence order is in force with respect to the child, has the consent of each of the persons in whose favour the order was made;

(ii) in any case where the child is in the care of a local authority, has the consent of that authority; or

(iii) in any other case, has the consent of each of those (if any) who have parental responsibility for the child.

The court can make this order of its own initiative in family proceedings, section 14A(6)(b) of the CA 1989.

Local authorities must make special guardianship services available (including counselling, mediation and resources which may include cash assistance) under section 14F of the CA 1989 and regulation 3 of the Special Guardianship Regulations 2005, SI 2005/1109.

For the distinction between the effects of special guardianship and a residence order, see *Birmingham City Council v R* [2006] EWCA Civ 1748, [2007] 1 FLR 564, and for a contrast with adoption, see *Re S (Adoption Order or Special Guardianship Order)* [2007] EWCA Civ 54, [2007] 1 FLR 819.

The order can be discharged on the application of the birth parents, but is not to be discharged unless there is a significant change of circumstances since the order was made, section 14(D)(5) of the CA 1989. See *Re G (Special Guardianship Order: Leave to Discharge)* [2010] EWCA Civ 300, [2010] All ER D 127. Also, see *K (Children) v Sheffield City Council* [2011] EWCA Civ 365, where the Court of Appeal made a special guardianship order, with a section 91(14) direction attached to it.

In relation to an application for a special guardianship order applied for during care proceedings, the child may have the benefit of the existing children's guardian. If the child is already subject to a care order, then the child may have the benefit of the previous children's guardian. The court can appoint a children's guardian if the court considers that it is in the child's interests, rule 16.2 of the FPR 2010. If so, the guardian will be appointed under rule 16.4.

3.5.6   Parental responsibility, surrogacy, and the Human Fertilisation and Embryology Act 2008

This is a complex area and has developed further with the HFEA 2008.

Some of the key provisions surrounding 'parenthood' are set out below at 3.5.7, and cover the situation when the surrogate mother is the child's genetic mother, or was impregnated with an embryo, or eggs.

The effect of section 42 of the HFEA 2008 is that if the child's mother is one who was in a civil partnership, at the time of her having had an embryo, sperm and eggs placed in her, or at the time of her undergoing artificial insemination: if her partner has agreed to this procedure, that partner will then be treated as the child's second parent (this is subject to the provisions relating to the legitimacy of the child, or if the child is through adoption, not treated as the women's child, see section 45(2) and (4)).

Under sections 43 and 44 of the HFEA 2008, there is a provision for situations where the child's mother is in a relationship with another woman, and the two women are *not* civil partners at the time of the procedure. These sections provide that if the child is born as a result of the provision of licensed treatment services in the UK, then if both women consent to the procedure (and subject to section 45(2) and (4) – see above), the non-biological mother is regarded in law as the child's second parent.

Section 2(11A) of the CA 1989 has the effect that where a child has a parent under either section 42 or section 43 of the HFEA 2008 (provided that the second female was the civil partner of the biological mother at the time of the child's birth, or was the civil partner of the child's biological mother at any time ending with the child's birth, pursuant to section 1(3) of the Family Law Reform Act 1987), then the child's biological mother and the other parent shall both have parental responsibility for the child.

What if the man is not the child's genetic father? Can he be treated as the child's father under the law? Under section 35(1) of the HFEA 2008, if the mother was married to her husband (who does not provide the sperm) at the time when the mother has placed into her the embryo, or sperm and eggs, or she undergoes artificial insemination, then provided that her husband consented to this process, he is treated as the child's father.

Consider section 36 of the HFEA 2008 – this has the effect that if the woman has had the child born to her through the same process as referred to above under section 35, but the man and woman have given written notice to the effect that they consent to the man being treated as the child's father, then provided the process occurs in the UK, through a licensed provider, the man will be treated as the child's father, even though he had not provided his sperm. This, however, is subject to the presumption of legitimacy, and if the child, by virtue of adoption, is not treated as that man's child.

3.5.7 Parental orders under section 54 of the Human Fertilisation and Embryology Act 2008

The HFEA 2008 allows a couple who have agreed with a surrogate mother to commission the birth of a child to apply under section 54 of the HFEA 2008 for a parental order that they be treated in law as the parents of that child.

The conditions on the making of a parental order include that:

- the applicants are aged 18 or over, and they must be domiciled in the UK, the Channel Islands, or the Isle of Man, at the time of the application;

- the surrogate mother who carried the child must not be one of the applicants;

- the gametes of at least one of the applicants must have been used, so as to bring about the creation of the embryo;

- the applicants must be married, civil partners, or are living in an enduring family relationship, and are not within the prohibited degrees of relationship to each other;

- the application must normally be made within six months of the birth of the child (subject to section 54(1) of the HFEA 2008);

- the birth mother was a surrogate mother and that she and the father (if he has parental responsibility for the child, see para 3.4.1) agree to the making of the order. The agreement is to be given after six weeks from the child's birth. The court can dispense with agreement in specified circumstances;

- the child was living with the applicants at the time of the application;

- no money or benefit has been handed over save for reasonable expenses incurred;

- any other person who is a parent of the child (but who is not one of the applicants) agreed to the making of the order, unless they cannot be traced.

4 *Every Child Matters*: Child Protection Procedures in Health and Social Work

Current child protection procedures are formed to operate within the framework of the Children Act 1989 (CA 1989) and the Children Act 2004, underpinning the *Every Child Matters: Change for Children* programme which includes the provisions for the establishment of Local Safeguarding Children Boards (LSCBs).

The CA 1989 and Children Act 2004 apply to both England and Wales, but *Every Child Matters* is a policy applicable only in England and there are some variations in Wales. For example, the *Working Together* (2010) guidance referred to below does not apply in Wales which has its own *All Wales Child Protection Procedures*. A guide to the relevant Welsh legislation and guidance is published by the Care Council for Wales and is available at www.ccwales.org.uk/child-law/.

The child protection procedures for England are set out in a number of publications. They are all accessible at www.education.gov.uk.

The main publication is *Working Together to Safeguard Children: A guide to inter-agency working to safeguard and promote the welfare of children* (DCSF, 2010), referred to below as *Working Together*. This forms part of a suite of documents which underpin *Every Child Matters*. The Department of Education website, www.education.gov.uk, has useful information and is worth visiting at regular intervals to see the new publications added, including:

- *Progress report: Moving towards a child centred system* (DfE 2012).

- *National Action Plan to tackle child abuse linked to faith or belief* (DfE 2012).

- *Support and Aspiration: A new approach to special educational needs and disability* (DfE 2012).

- *Statutory guidance on the roles and responsibilities of the Director of Children's Services and the Lead Member for Children's Services* (DfE, 2012).

- *Safeguarding Children and Young People who may be Affected by Gang Activity* (DCSF, 2010).

- *Safeguarding children who may have been trafficked – Practice guidance* (DCSF, 2011).

The CA 1989 is clarified and explained by the volumes of *The Children Act 1989 Guidance and Regulations* published by the DCSF and available, along with new publications, at www.education.gov.uk. These volumes of guidance and *Working Together*, Part 1 are all mandatory guidelines issued under section 7 of the Local Authority Social Services Act 1970. Local authorities must follow that guidance, unless local circumstances indicate exceptional reasons that justify a variation, and any departure from it must be justified in respect of any complaints procedure or judicial review.

Working Together, Chapters 3, 4, 7 and 8 are also issued under section 16 of the Children Act 2004, which states that Children's Services Authorities and each of the statutory partners must, in exercising their functions relating to an LSCB, have regard to any guidance given to them for the purpose by the Secretary of State. This means that they must take the guidance into account and, if they decide to depart from it, have clear reasons for doing so.

Other key policy and planning documents relating to *Every Child Matters* include:

- *The National Service Framework for Children, Young People and Maternity Services* (DoH, DfES, 2004), which sets out a ten-year programme to stimulate long-term and sustained improvement in children's health and wellbeing.

- *Every Child Matters: Change for Children – Young People and Drugs* (DfES, 2005), which gives guidance on co-operation and joint planning to counter drug misuse.

- *Promoting the Educational Achievement of Looked After Children: Statutory Guidance for Local Authorities* (DCSF, 2010), which sets out the implications of the new duty in the Children Act 2004 for local authorities, strategic planning, joint area reviews and day-to-day working practices.

- *Inspections of safeguarding and looked after children services: framework for inspection and guidance for local authorities and partners* (Ofsted, 2010), which sets out the principles to be applied by an inspectorate or commission assessing any children's service, and defines the key judgements which, where appropriate and practical, inspections will seek to make. It is available at www.ofsted.gov.uk.

- *Information sharing: Guidance for practitioners and managers* (DCSF, 2008) and the supporting materials, which are for everyone who works with children and young people, and explain when and how information can be shared legally and professionally.

Each local authority, district council, NHS body and the police, probation and prison services along with Secure Offending Services, Connexions and Youth Offending Teams have a duty under section 11 of the Children Act 2004 to discharge their functions with regard to the need to safeguard and promote the welfare of children. See *Making Arrangements to Safeguard and Promote the Welfare of Children* (DfES, 2005).

Working Together, Chapter 3 covers the role of the LSCB in detail. See also the Local Safeguarding Children Boards Regulations 2006, SI 2006/90.

See the *Codes of Practice for Social Care Workers and Employers of Social Care Workers* (GSCC, 2010) (available at www.nationalarchives.gov.uk). From 1 August 2012, regulation of social workers devolves from the General Social Care Council (GSCC) regionally as follows:

- In England, to the newly-renamed Health & Care Professions Council (HCPC), www.hpc-uk.org.

- In Scotland, to the Scottish Social Services Council, www.sssc.uk.com.

- In Wales, to the Care Council for Wales, www.ccwales.org.uk.

- In Northern Ireland, to the Care Council for Northern Ireland Social Care Council, www.niscc.info.

Under the new arrangements, social care workers in Northern Ireland will benefit from better access to supervision and more flexible working arrangements. Northern Ireland's first ever strategy for social work proposes to strengthen the capacity of the country's 5,000-strong workforce, improve services and build leadership within the profession over the next ten years. Northern Ireland was the first devolved administration to introduce an assessed year in employment for newly qualified social workers and establish a principal social work practitioner grade.

See the NISCC website for key recommendations for Northern Ireland, which include:

- focusing on prevention and early intervention, as well as protection and safeguarding;

- developing a regional out-of-hours social work service;

- introducing flexible working arrangements by extending opening hours and exploring better use of technology;

- creating new standards for social work employers and promoting access to professional supervision;

- developing a workload weighting system for social work in adult services, building on experience in children's services;

- helping social workers to effectively represent the profession in the media.

LSCBs are multi-disciplinary groups comprising senior representatives from local organisations and agencies involved in the *Every Child Matters* programme. Each LSCB should develop local policies and procedures, and ensure co-ordination and co-operation between agencies in the implementation of child protection procedures in its locality. Each organisation and agency retains its own line of accountability for operational work. Practitioners should be aware of the policies and procedures developed by the local LSCB in the area in which they work.

4.1 Hierarchy within social services departments

Each social services department will use terminology that is likely to vary geographically. The head of social services may be called the Director of Social Services, supported by one or more Assistant Directors, each of whom usually has an administrative responsibility related either to an area of work, or to a geographical area. The *Statutory guidance on the roles and responsibilities of the Director of Children's Services and the Lead Member for Children's Services* (DfE, 2012) is available at www.education.gov.uk.

The local authority children's social care department deals with child protection. Social services departments are generally divided into task-related divisions, for example, child care, community care, etc. One Assistant Director may have the responsibility for child care, which may or may not include adoption.

Out in the field, the frontline work may be divided into geographical areas, and then sub-divided into specific tasks, headed by a person in a managerial role, perhaps called the Divisional Manager or District Manager. The work is usually carried out by social work teams.

4.2 Referral procedures and preliminary investigations

See *Working Together*, Chapter 5 for detailed guidance on referral procedures, and see also Figure 1.

Figure 1   Local authority referral procedures

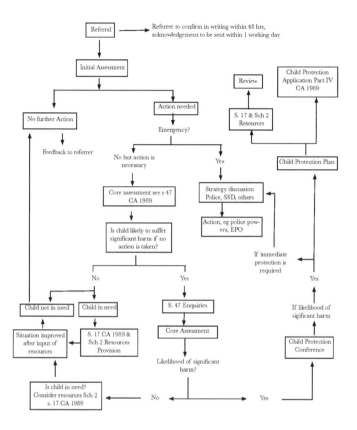

The local LSCB should ensure that organisations and agencies have contact lists of addresses and telephone numbers for referral. A member of the public concerned about a child should contact the police, the local authority children's social care department or the NSPCC. The police will usually either use their powers under section 46 of the CA 1989 in an emergency or refer the matter to social services.

Social services in each area appoint a 'duty officer' to take referrals. The duty officer will note the information given, ask further details to establish the name, whereabouts and circumstances of the child, and request information about the person making the referral if appropriate.

Professionals referring concerns to social services are expected to confirm the referral in writing within 48 hours. This is to ensure that referrals are properly recorded, and not missed or, for other reasons, not followed up. The Common Assessment Framework provides a structure for the written referral. *Working Together* recommends that at the end of any discussion or dialogue about a child, the referrer (whether a professional or a member of the public or family) and the local authority children's social care department should be clear about proposed action, timescales and who will be taking it, or that no further action will be taken. The decision should be recorded by the local authority children's social care department and by the referrer (if a professional in another service). The local authority children's social care department should acknowledge a written referral within one working day of receiving it. If the referrer has not received an acknowledgement within three working days, he or she should contact the local authority children's social care again.

When responding to referrals from a member of the public rather than another professional, the local authority children's social care department should bear in mind that personal information about referrers, including identifying details, should only be disclosed to third parties (including subject families and other agencies) with the consent of the referrer. In all cases where the police are involved, the decision about when to inform the parents (about referrals from third parties) will have a bearing on the conduct of police investigations.

Where no further action is to be taken by the local authority, feedback should be provided to the referrer, who should be told of this decision and the reasons for making it. We should emphasise here the important role of the Independent Reviewing Officer (IRO) at the end of proceedings. The IRO is appointed by the local authority to regularly review the implementation of the care plan for all children in local authority care, bearing in mind the needs and welfare of the child. In theory at least, the IRO now takes on the independent monitoring and oversight role which was previously fulfilled by the guardian and solicitor for the child. It is therefore important that this is borne in mind at the end of proceedings and that the children's guardian considers whether he or she needs to feed back to or liaise with the IRO before closing his or her files.

A child at risk of significant harm is, by definition, a child in need. In most cases, a child in need would remain at home, helped by the provision of appropriate services, resources and advice for the family. However, some children need greater levels of protection. The local authority must therefore carry out an initial assessment in accordance with the *Framework for the assessment of children in need and their families* (DoH, 2000) (the *Assessment Framework*) and decide quickly whether it is necessary to seek emergency protection, child assessment or any other CA 1989 order. See Chapter 16 for details of the assessment process.

The local authority immediately trawls for information from the referrer, police, general practitioner and others to whom the family is known. This is known as undertaking 'safeguarding checks'.

4.2.1 Involving the child

Working Together requires professionals to elicit the child's wishes and feelings unless this is not possible or practicable (paras 1.17–1.18, page 33 and para 1.30, page 37), expects effective information sharing between professionals (para 2.12–2.14, pages 43–44) and encourages co-operation between professionals and the child's family in child protection (para 2.23, page 47). In addition, child protection should be child-centred (para 5.5, pages 133–134).

The child should be seen (alone when appropriate) by the lead social worker in addition to all other professionals who have a responsibility for the child's welfare. His or her welfare should be kept sharply in focus in all work with the child and family. The significance of seeing and observing the child cannot be overstated. The child should be spoken and listened to, and their wishes and feelings ascertained, taken into account (having regard to their age and understanding) and recorded when making decisions about the provision of services. Some of the worst failures of the system have occurred when professionals have lost sight of the child and concentrated instead on their relationship with the adults.

4.2.2 Involving families

The importance of developing a co-operative working relationship is emphasised, so that parents or caregivers feel respected and informed, they believe staff are being open and honest with them and, in turn, they are confident about providing vital information about their child, themselves and their circumstances. The consent of children or their parents or caregivers should be obtained when sharing information, unless to do so would place the child at risk of significant harm. Similarly, decisions should also be made with their agreement, whenever possible, unless to do so would place the child at risk of significant harm (para 5.5, page 135).

However, in certain circumstances, involving parents in the discussion is not possible or safe for the child (para 5.67, page 157).

Exceptionally, a joint enquiry/investigation team may need to speak to a suspected child victim without the knowledge of the parent or caregiver. Relevant circumstances would include the possibility that a child would be threatened or otherwise coerced into silence, a strong likelihood that important evidence would be destroyed or that the child in question did not wish the parent to be involved at that stage and is competent to take that decision. Possible outcomes of an initial assessment are:

(a)   no further action needs to be taken;

(b)   protection can be achieved by working in co-operation with the parents and provision of services, etc.;

(c)   section 47 enquiries and core assessment required;

(d)   child protection conference is required;

(e)   urgent court proceedings are necessary.

4.3   Child protection conferences

Child protection conferences bring together the child and their family members with those professionals most involved with them. *Working Together* provides detailed guidance for child protection conferences, reviews and decision-making processes in paragraphs 5.80–5.135. See Figure 2 for the child protection conference process.

4.3.1   Purpose

The purpose of the child protection conference is to:

•   bring together the family, child and professionals most involved and analyse evidence about the needs of the child and the parents' or carers' capacity to respond to the child's needs;

•   ensure the child's safety and promote the child's health and development in the context of his or her wider family and environment. If the child is at continuing risk of significant harm, the conference must decide what future action is required to safeguard and promote the welfare of the child.

4.3.2   Who should be invited to a child protection conference?

The parents, carers and child (if of sufficient age and maturity) should be invited. The professionals invited should include all those who can make a significant contribution to the discussion. Those who are invited but cannot attend should be invited to submit a written report.

Figure 2   Process of child protection conference

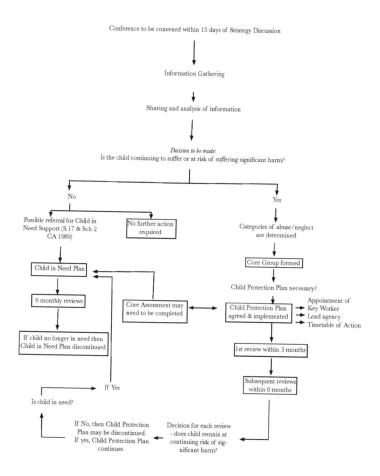

Invitees should include:

- the child or his or her representative;
- family members (including wider family where appropriate);
- local authority children's social care staff involved with the child and family;
- foster carers, residential care staff;
- professionals involved with the child and family (medical, support, education, etc.);

those involved in investigations (e.g. the police);

- experts, if appropriate;
- legal services;
- representative of the NSPCC or armed forces, where relevant.

4.3.3 Documents

The child protection conference should have before it documents including:

- a local authority written report, including any information obtained from the safeguarding checks;
- a chronology of significant events and professional contact with the family;
- information on the capacity of the parents/carers to meet the child's needs and provide protection;
- the expressed views, wishes and feelings of the child, parents and family members;
- an analysis of the implications of the information gained.

The child and parents should be provided with a copy of the local authority report before the conference and the contents explained appropriately. They should be helped to think about and convey what they want to say to the conference.

4.3.4 Decisions to be made and actions to be taken

(a) Is the child at continuing risk of significant harm?

The test is one of the following:

    (i)   the child can be shown to have suffered ill-treatment or impairment of health or development as a result of physical, emotional or sexual abuse or neglect, and professional judgement is that further ill-treatment or impairment are likely; or

    (ii)   professional judgement, substantiated by the findings of enquiries in this individual case or by research evidence, is that the child is likely to suffer ill-treatment or the impairment of health or development as a result of physical, emotional or sexual abuse; or

    (iii) neglect.

(b)   The child may be a child in need (but not subject to a child protection plan) and a child in need plan can be drawn up and reviewed every six months.

(c)   If the child is at continuing risk of significant harm, then inter-agency help will be required, delivered through a child protection plan.

(d)   If a child protection plan is required, then the Child Protection Conference chair will determine the category (or categories) of abuse (physical, sexual, emotional or neglect).

(e)   The child protection plan must be agreed in detail.

(f)   The Conference must agree on the appointment of a key worker, and establish the core group of professionals and family members who will implement the plan.

(g)   The responsibilities of the core group members and family must be agreed upon.

(h)   The provision of resources for child/family by the agencies must be agreed upon.

It should be noted that it is not good practice for a child to remain subject to a child protection plan for long periods of time.

The chair is usually employed by social services but is independent, with no line-management responsibility for case work with the family involved. Attendance at child protection conferences is by invitation, which should include all professionals involved with the family, the parents and carers of the child and the child if of sufficient age and understanding. The chair should ensure that invitees are made welcome and comfortable, with refreshments, toilet facilities and other necessities being provided. Minutes should be taken, and decisions recorded. Exclusions should be by the conference chair, and only when justified, in an adversarial role, see *Handbook of Best Practice in Children Act Cases* (Children Act Advisory Committee, 1997), *Representation of Children in Public Law Proceedings* (Law Society, 2006), and *The SFLA Guide to Good Practice for Solicitors Acting for Children* (SFLA, 6th edn, 2002).

A review of the child protection plan should regularly follow a child protection conference. The first should take place within three months of the conference. The following reviews should take place at no more than six-monthly intervals. Extra reviews may be convened at the request of other professionals.

The provision of resources under section 17 of and Schedule 2 to the CA 1989 is a statutory duty for a child in need (see para 4.6) and should not depend on registration.

4.3.5 Categories of abuse

Emotional abuse

Actual or likely severe adverse effect upon the emotional or behavioural development of a child caused by persistent or severe emotional ill treatment or rejection. All abuse involves some form of emotional ill treatment. This category should be used where it is the sole or the main form of the abuse.

Neglect

Persistent or severe neglect of a child, failure to protect from danger, extreme failure to carry out aspects of care resulting in impairment of child's health or development, including non-organic failure to thrive.

Physical injury

Actual or likely physical injury to a child, and failure to prevent physical injury or suffering, including deliberate poisoning, suffocation, etc. and Munchhausen's syndrome by proxy.

Sexual abuse

Actual or likely sexual exploitation of a child or adolescent. The child may be dependent and/or developmentally immature.

4.3.6 Criteria for discontinuance of the child protection plan

- No longer a continuing risk of significant harm requiring safeguarding.

- Child and/or family moved permanently to another area.

- Requirement that the new area local authority takes over the responsibility for future management of the case within 15 days.

- Child reaches 18, or dies.

4.4 Assessment of risk

See *Working Together to Safeguard Children* (DCSF, 2010) (*Working Together*); *Framework for the Assessment of Risk* (DCSF, 2000); *Assessing children in need and their families: Practice Guidance* (DoH, 2000); the range of *Initial and Core Assessment Records* (DCSF, 2000) for children of different age groups; and the *Family Assessment Pack of Questionnaires and Scales* (DCSF, 2000). See, also, more detailed discussion in Chapter 16.

Local authorities on referral assess the likelihood of significant harm to a child, that is, evaluation of the potential risk to the child should she remain within her family or the risk to the child if removed from home. After registration there should follow a carefully planned and structured comprehensive assessment within the child protection plan, to gain a better understanding of the child's situation.

Comprehensive assessments require co-operation of agencies and professionals involved with the family. Professionals involved should be asked about how long they will need, the venue, timing and personnel to carry out the assessment – all must be clearly agreed.

4.5 Child protection plan

Child protection plans should not be confused with the care plans which are required in care proceedings; see Chapters 7 and 16.

Working Together, paragraphs 5.113–5.135 address the formulation and implementation of child protection plans made between family and professionals. Once the plan is agreed, each person should take responsibility to implement his or her part of it and to communicate with the others involved, with contingency provisions for crises and regular review. Parents and older children should have a copy of the plan, be informed of the nature and purposes of the interventions offered and confirm that they agree with the plan and are willing to work with it. If the family has particular preferences about the protection work which are not accepted by the professionals, then the professionals' reasons should be explained to the family, together with the right of the family to complain or to make representations.

The child protection plan should:

- be in writing, in clear language, setting out the expectations and responsibilities of each party;

- describe the identifiable needs of the child and what therapeutic services are required;

- include specific, achievable, child-focused outcomes intended to safeguard and promote the welfare of the child;

- include realistic strategies and specific actions to achieve the planned outcomes;

- include a contingency plan to be followed if circumstances change significantly and require prompt action;

- clearly identify roles and responsibilities of professionals and family members, including the nature and frequency of contact by professionals with children and family members;

- lay down points at which progress will be reviewed, and the means by which progress will be judged; and

- set out clearly the roles and responsibilities of those professionals with routine contact with the child – e.g. health visitors, GPs and teachers – as well as those professionals providing specialist or targeted support to the child and family.

The plan should be explained, and agreed with the child and the family.

4.6 Child and Family Court Advisory Support Service

Following a consultation paper in 1998, the government made radical changes to the family court advisory system, unifying the Children's Guardian and Reporting Officer Service, the Family Court Welfare Service and the Children's Branch of the Official Solicitor's Department to form the Children and Family Court Advisory and Support Service (CAFCASS), with the motto 'children first'.

Information can be obtained from the CAFCASS government website, www.cafcass.gov.uk and at the website of NAGALRO (Professional Association for Children's Guardians, Family Court Advisers and Independent Social Workers), www.nagalro.com.

CAFCASS's functions are to:

- safeguard and promote the welfare of children who are the subject of family proceedings;

- give advice to any court about any application made to it in such proceedings;

- make provision for children to be represented in such proceedings;

- provide information, advice and other support for children and their families.

The CAFCASS officer (who might be a CAFCASS employee or may sometimes be a self-employed contractor) is appointed by the court and can be referred to by this general title. CAFCASS officers have different roles in private and public law proceedings:

- children's guardians, who are appointed to safeguard the interests of a child who is the subject of specified proceedings under the CA 1989 or who is the subject of adoption proceedings;

- parental order reporters, who are appointed to investigate and report to the court on circumstances relevant under the Human Fertilisation and Embryology Act 1990;

- children and family reporters, who prepare welfare reports for the court in relation to applications under section 8 of the CA 1989 (private law proceedings, including applications for residence and contact). Increasingly they also work with families at the stage of their initial application to the court;

- CAFCASS officers can also be appointed to provide support under a family assistance order under the CA 1989. (Local authority officers can also be appointed for this purpose.)

The CAFCASS officer has a statutory right in public law cases to access and take copies of local authority records relating to the child concerned and any application under the CA 1989. That power also extends to other records that relate to the child and the wider functions of the local authority or records held by an authorised body (e.g. the NSPCC) that relate to that child.

Where a CAFCASS officer has been appointed by the court as children's guardian and the matter before the court relates to specified proceedings (specified proceedings include public law proceedings; applications for contact; residence, specific issue and prohibited steps orders that have become particularly difficult can also be specified proceedings), they should be invited to all formal planning meetings convened by the local authority in respect of the child. This includes statutory reviews of children who are accommodated or looked after, child protection conferences and relevant Adoption Panel Meetings. The conference chair should ensure that all those attending such meetings, including the child and any family members, understand the role of the CAFCASS officer.

It should be noted that the independence of the children's guardian from CAFCASS was clarified by the President of the Family Division in 2011, in *A County Council v K and Others* [2011] EWHC 1672 (Fam). The President stressed the independence of children's guardian and the personal nature of their appointment as enshrined in section 41 of the CA 1989. He went on to set out guidance as to what should happen in care proceedings when there is an irrevocable disagreement between CAFCASS and the individual guardian appointed by the court under section 41.

4.7   Local authority duty to promote welfare of children in its area

Section 17 of and Schedule 2 to the CA 1989 impose on local authorities a duty to promote the welfare of children in their area, with special provision for 'children in need' and children under five years old. Schedule 2 to the CA 1989 provides a list of the services and resources that may be provided. Local authorities must now implement the recommendations of *Every Child Matters* and comply with the wealth of guidance discussed earlier in the first paragraphs in this chapter.

Local authorities must provide family centres as appropriate for children in their area with counselling advice or guidance, occupational, social or recreational activities, Schedule 2, paragraph 9(1) to the CA 1989. Local authorities may provide recreational facilities, section 19(1) of the Local Government (Miscellaneous Provisions) Act 1976. Section 18 of the CA 1989 requires provision of day care for children under school age and for those of school age outside school hours or in the holidays. Section 17(6) of the CA 1989 authorises financial help in exceptional circumstances.

4.7.1   Duty to investigate potential or actual harm to child

Section 47 of the CA 1989 requires a local authority, when informed that a child who lives or is found in its area is subject to emergency or police protection, or has reasonable cause to suspect that the child is suffering, or is likely to suffer significant harm, to 'make such enquiries as they consider necessary to enable them to decide whether they should take any action to safeguard or promote the child's welfare'. See *Working Together*, Chapters 3, 5 and 6.

The enquiries are intended to establish whether the authority should make any application to the court or exercise its powers under the CA 1989. The authority should consider providing accommodation for a child subject to an emergency protection order if it is not already doing so, section 47(3)(b) of the CA 1989; and, if the child is in police protection, then the authority should consider applying for an emergency protection order, section 47(3)(c). Enquiries may be made with the child's school, carers, and others. Refusal of access to the child or denial of information may justify an application for an emergency protection order. The local authority is under a duty to consider and timetable a review, if no present action is required. If action is necessary then the authority is under a duty to take it, section 47(8).

4.7.2 Local authority duty to children in need

Section 17(1) of the CA 1989 imposes on local authorities a twofold duty:

> (a) to safeguard and promote the welfare of children within their area who are in need; and

> (b) ... to promote the upbringing of such children by their families,

> by providing a range and level of services appropriate to those children's needs.

Under section 17, those services are free to families on income support or family credit, but otherwise may be subject to means-related contributions.

Section 17(10) defines a child being in need if:

> (a) he is unlikely to achieve or maintain, or to have the opportunity of achieving or maintaining, a reasonable standard of health or development without the provision for him of services by the local authority ...;

> (b) his health or development is likely to be significantly impaired, or further impaired, without the provision for him of such services; or

> (c) he is disabled.

The services can be provided to the child direct or to the family for the benefit of the child. Local authorities should publish information about the services in their area. Services are listed in Schedule 2 to the CA 1989.

'Health', 'development' and 'disabled' are all defined in the CA 1989. The term 'disabled' was adopted to conform with the wording of the National Assistance Act 1948. Under section 17(6) of the CA 1989 assistance may be financial in exceptional circumstances or in kind.

4.7.3 Services for children and their families

Schedule 2, paragraph 8 to the CA 1989 lists services which local authorities should provide for children living with their families:

- advice, guidance and counselling;

- occupational, social, cultural or recreational activities;

- home help (which may include laundry facilities);

- facilities for, or assistance with, travelling to and from home for the purpose of taking advantage of any other service provided under this Act or similar service (includes travel for contact purposes); and

- assistance to enable the child concerned and his family to have a holiday.

4.7.4   Duty to children under five

There is power under section 18 of the CA 1989 to provide day care for children under school age. *Guidance and Regulations*, Volume 2 *Family Support, Day Care and Educational Provision for Young Children* is helpful in giving ideas to practitioners about the nature and standards of the provision to be expected. Watch for new developments in day care and child minding issues, for example, policies on smacking.

4.7.5   Compliance with court order to investigate child's circumstances, section 37 of the Children Act 1989

Under section 37 of the CA 1989, in any 'family proceedings' in which a question arises as to the welfare of any child, if it appears to the court that it may be appropriate for a care or supervision order to be made, the court may order the local authority to investigate the child's circumstances. The local authority then has to consider whether it should apply for a care or supervision order, provide services for the family or take any other action with respect to the child, section 37(2). If the local authority decides not to seek an order, its reasons must be reported to the court within eight weeks, as must the services provided or to be provided, and any other action taken or proposed with respect to the child, section 37(3) and (4). The local authority may also need to review the situation and set a date for such a review, section 37(6).

4.7.6   'Looked after' children: responsibility of the local authority

Local authorities may provide accommodation for certain children in need, whether voluntarily at the request of the child' parents or carers; under a care order or for assessment purposes, or otherwise by order of the court, for example where the child is required to live in secure accommodation.

There is strict regulation of the standards of care for children who are accommodated or 'looked after' by local authorities – this includes children who are provided with accommodation by the local authority on a voluntary basis under section 20 of the CA 1989.

Some children are provided with accommodation under section 59 of the CA 1989 by voluntary organisations. The local authorities are also responsible for oversight of the standards of this care.

For all 'looked after' children, care plans and regular reviews must be made under the Care Planning, Placement and Case Review (England) Regulations 2010, SI 2010/959 and an independent reporting officer appointed to oversee the welfare of the child.

5 Emergency Protection Orders

Emergency protection orders are available under section 44 of the Children Act 1989 (CA 1989), as amended by section 52 of and Schedule 6, paragraph 3 to the Family Law Act 1996. They are designed for situations when a child needs urgent removal to a safe place or to be retained in a safe place, such as a hospital. These orders may also be used to obtain access to a child in danger, when urgent action is necessary and/or to exclude a named person from a dwelling house or defined area in which the child lives, and they may include a power of arrest. An order may be made in respect of any child under 18 years of age living or found within the jurisdiction of the court.

5.1 Effects of order

The order gives parental responsibility for the child to the applicant, section 44(5) of the CA 1989. It authorises the applicant to remove or retain the child, section 44(4)(b); and operates as a direction to anyone in a position to do so, to produce the child, section 44(4)(a). Under section 44(15) it is a criminal offence to obstruct the applicant in the exercise of his powers under the order.

The order has wide powers, and may contain any or all of these directions:

- authorising doctor, nurse or health visitor to accompany the applicant to carry out the order, section 45(12) of the CA 1989;

- for child to have contact with any named person, section 44(6)(a);

- for medical or psychiatric examination of the child, section 44(6)(b);

- requirement to disclose information concerning whereabouts of the child, section 48(1);

- authorisation to enter premises and search for the child, section 48(3);

- authorisation to search for another child in the same premises, section 48(4);

- issue of warrant to police officer to assist the applicant, section 48(9);

- authorisation for nurse, doctor, or health visitor to accompany police, section 48(11);

- exclusion requirement under section 44(A)(2) requiring a named person to leave and remain away from the dwelling house or area in which the child lives;

- undertaking in respect of an exclusion requirement section 44(B); and

- power of arrest in relation to an exclusion requirement section 44(A)(5) and (8).

5.2 Duration

Emergency protection orders last initially for eight days, renewable for a further seven days, section 45(1) of the CA 1989.

There are some exceptions to this general rule, including the following:

- if the order would expire on a public holiday – first order goes to noon on the next day, section 45(2) of the CA 1989;

- if the child was in police protection (duration 76 hours maximum) before emergency protection order, and the designated police officer is the applicant on behalf of the local authority, the emergency protection order commences from beginning of police protection, section 45(3).

5.3 Grounds for application

The grounds to be proved depend upon who the applicant is.

Since anyone can apply for this order there is a general ground, which is that if the intention is to remove a child to a safe place, the applicant must satisfy the court that there is reasonable cause to believe that the child will suffer significant harm if not removed to accommodation provided by him, and also that there is suitable accommodation available for the child, section 44(1)(A)(i) of the CA 1989.

If the applicant intends to retain the child in a safe place, then it must be proved that there is reasonable cause to believe that the child is likely to suffer significant harm unless retained in a safe place, section 44(1)(a)(ii). The grounds can be established on the existence of present harm or a prognosis indicating a future risk to the child. For the definition of 'significant harm', see Chapter 7, paras 7.2–7.4.

A local authority applicant has an additional ground. It can satisfy the court that during enquiries made under section 47 of the CA 1989 about a child in its area, access to the child requested by a person authorised to seek it is being refused unreasonably, and that the access is required as a matter of urgency, section 44(1)(b)(ii). The question of reasonable refusal is a matter for the court. See *The Children Act 1989 Guidance and Regulations* (DCSF), Volume 1 *Court Orders* for examples.

If the application is made by an authorised officer of the local authority or an 'authorised person' (currently only the NSPCC), there is either the general ground, or an additional ground, that the applicant has reasonable cause to suspect that the child is suffering or is likely to suffer significant harm, that the applicant is making enquiries as to the child's welfare, that access to the child is being unreasonably refused, and access is urgently needed, section 44(1) of the CA 1989.

The CA 1989 principles of the paramountcy of the welfare of the child, avoidance of delay and no order unless necessary for the welfare of the child apply. However, the application is not 'family proceedings' within the meaning of section 8(4) of the CA 1989 and so the 'welfare checklist' does not apply.

5.4   Practice and procedure

5.4.1   Application

Emergency protection orders may be sought by any person. Usually, however, the applicant will be an 'authorised officer' of the local authority or, less commonly, applications may be made by an 'authorised person' (currently only the NSPCC) or 'a designated officer' of the police.

The application should be made in the family proceedings court (FPC), unless the local authority has been directed to investigate under section 37 of the CA 1989 or there are proceedings pending in another court. In these exceptional cases the application can be made in the relevant court, Article 5 of the Allocation and Transfer of Proceedings Order 2008, SI 2008/28. Application is on form C1, together with form C11. Both forms are contained within the list of forms in PD 5A accompanying the Family Procedure Rules 2010, SI 2010/2955 (FPR 2010). The procedure is governed by the FPR 2010, and in particular Part 12, as well as the accompanying PD 12C.

Applications for extensions should be made to the court which made the original order, Proceedings commenced in the FPC can be transferred sideways to another FPC, but not upwards, Article 14 of the Allocation and Transfer of Proceedings Order 2008. The application should name the child and, if this is not possible, it should give a description of the child for identification purposes.

A children's guardian will be appointed by the court to oversee the welfare of the child and to advise the court on the child's best interests, see sections 41–42 of the CA 1989 and Chapter 15, para 15.1.

5.4.2   Respondents

The forms of notice on form C6 plus a copy of the application, with the hearing date endorsed on it, must be served on respondents, together with notice of the date and place of the hearing.

Those listed below are automatically considered respondents to the application:

- everyone with parental responsibility for the child;

- if there is a care order, all those who had parental responsibility immediately prior to the care order;

- the child if of sufficient age and understanding.

See rule 12.3 of the FPR 2010. Others may be joined as respondents, and respondents may be removed by direction of the court, see rules 4.3 and 12.3(3).

5.4.3   Applications made without notice (previously referred to as *ex parte* applications)

Reference is to be made to the 'interpretation section' in Part 2 of the FPR 2010 in terms of usage of terms such as '*ex parte*' and 'leave'. Applications for an emergency protection order should be made to the FPC, and only to the county court or High Court if there are ongoing proceedings in that court. An application for an emergency protection order may be made without notice but in the FPC, the permission of the justice's clerk must first be obtained. Applications may be made by telephone. Any order that is made would be expected to be served upon each respondent within 48 hours of the order being made (rule 12.6 and PD 12E accompanying the FPR 2010), although, in practice, it will usually be served on the same day that it was granted.

5.4.4 Notice

If an application is made on notice, form C6A, and the date, time and venue of the application must be given within one day of the hearing to:

- parents of the child without parental responsibility;

- any person caring for the child or with whom the child is living when the proceedings are commenced;

- a local authority providing accommodation for the child;

- a person providing a refuge under section 51 of the CA 1989, in which the child lives.

See PD 12C, paragraph 3.1 accompanying the FPR 2010.

5.4.5 Service

Service must be effected one day before the directions or application hearing, PD 12C, paragraph 12.1 accompanying the FPR 2010. It is important to note that in some cases of urgency, where the child has been born that same day and the local authority needs to seek an emergency protection order that same day and to do so 'on notice', it may seek to apply to abridge time for service to less than a day. Such a direction can be made pursuant to rule 4.1(3)(a).

5.4.6 Attendance

By rule 4.3(d) of the FPR 2010, the court can direct that the parties and/or their legal representatives must attend directions appointments and hearings unless otherwise directed by the court. If respondents fail to appear, the court may proceed in their absence. If applicants fail to attend, the court may refuse their application. Rule 4.3 provides that except where an enactment provides otherwise, the court may exercise its powers on an application, or of its own initiative.

5.5 Contact, accommodation and the rights of the child

5.5.1 Contact

The child must be allowed reasonable contact with:

- parents;

- those with parental responsibility for the child;

- anyone with whom the child was living before the order;

- anyone with a contact order under section 8 or section 34 of the CA 1989 in force in respect of the child, or anyone acting on their behalf;

- anyone with an order for access to the child, section 44(13).

The court can control the contact by directions within the emergency protection order. See section 44(6)(a) of the CA 1989.

In relation to contact between parents and babies/infants, see the significant case law set out in cases such as *Re M (Care Proceedings: Judicial Review)* [2003] EWHC 850 (Admin), [2003] 2 FLR 171, and *Kirklees MBC v S (Contact to new born babies)* [2006] 1 FLR 333.

5.5.2   Accommodation

The child has the right to accommodation provided, funded or arranged by the local authority, see in particular, the amendments to section 23 of the CA 1989, brought about by sections 8–9 of the Children and Young Persons Act 2008. Section 22 of the CA 1989 requires the local authority to provide accommodation, services and education for the child whom it is looking after. Section 22G of the CA 1989 requires the local authority to ensure that there is secure accommodation available where necessary for looked after children.

5.5.3   Rights of the child

The child has the right to be returned to his home once the danger has passed and the grounds for the order no longer subsist, section 44(10) of the CA 1989.

A child of sufficient age and understanding has the right to be consulted and informed about events that are happening. In particular, section 25B of the CA 1989 (brought in by section 10 of the Children and Young Persons Act 2008) should be considered, which requires the Independent Reviewing Officer to ensure that the ascertainable wishes and feelings of the chid are given appropriate consideration by the local authority.

The emergency protection order may include a direction about medical or psychiatric assessment of the child, section 44 of the CA 1989. The directions can order or prohibit examinations, either completely or without permission of the court. Directions for examination/assessment can include venue, personnel to be present and nomination of the person(s) to whom results should be given. A child of sufficient age and understanding has the right to make an informed refusal of medical or psychiatric assessment. A '*Gillick*-competent' child, or a young person over 16, may consent to or refuse medical treatment, see Chapter 12, paras 12.1 and 12.2.

5.6 Variation and discharge

There is no right of appeal against an emergency protection order, perhaps because of its short duration, see section 45(10) of the CA 1989. It can be challenged by an application to vary or to discharge the order.

The child, child's parents, those with parental responsibility for the child, and anyone with whom the child was living when the order was made, can make an application for variation or discharge, section 45(8) of the CA 1989.

Note that, previously, it was the case that there had to be a time lapse of 72 hours after the order 'without notice' before there could be a hearing of an application for discharge, section 45(9) of the CA 1989. However, this provision was revoked in April 2009 by section 30 of the Children and Young Persons Act 2008, so that it is possible to apply for discharge of the order even on the same day it was made.

The rules provide, however, that if a person has had notice of the original application for the emergency protection order, and has attended and opposed the application at the hearing, then there is no right to seek a discharge, section 45(11) of the CA 1989.

5.7 Exclusion requirement under emergency protection order

The local authority may wish to make arrangements for the removal of an alleged abuser as an alternative to an emergency removal of the child. Under Schedule 2, paragraph 5 to the CA 1989, the local authority has power to assist the alleged abuser in finding alternative accommodation.

Under section 44A(1)–(2) of the CA 1989, the court can make an exclusion requirement where:

> (a) there is reasonable cause to believe that if a person is excluded from the dwelling in which the child lives, the child will cease to suffer or cease to be likely to suffer, significant harm; and

> (b) another person living in the dwelling house (whether a parent of the child or some other person):

  (i) is able and willing and able to give to the child the care which it would be reasonable to expect a parent to give him, and

  (ii) consents to the exclusion requirement.

The consent can be given at court, orally or in writing.

A power of arrest can be attached to the exclusion requirement, under section 44A(5) of the CA 1989, and if an order is made, then (unless the person to whom it applies was given notice of the hearing and attended the court) the name of the person and that an order was made need to be announced in open court. See PD 12K, paragraph 1 accompanying the FPR 2010. Also, PD 12K, paragraph 3 provides that any order of committal made otherwise than in public, or in a courtroom open to the public, shall be announced in open court at the earliest opportunity. This may be either on the same day when the court proceeds to hear cases in open court, or where there is no further business in open court on that day, at the next listed sitting of the court. The announcement shall state: (a) the name of the person committed; (b) in general terms the nature of the contempt of the court in respect of which the order of committal has been made; and (c) the length of the period of committal.

5.7.1 Two notes of caution

- An undertaking from the person required to leave the dwelling house can be accepted instead of an exclusion order, but then no power of arrest can then be attached, section 44B(2) of the CA 1989.

- If the child is removed from the house to which an exclusion order or undertaking applies for a continuous period of more than 24 hours, the order or undertaking will cease to apply, section 44A(10) of the CA 1989. If an exclusion order is in force and the child is to be absent from the house for more than 24 hours for any reason which is known in advance, it would be wise to notify the court, and to seek appropriate directions.

5.8 How do 'without notice' orders and Article 6 of the ECHR fit together?

There are various procedural safeguards to ensure that these orders are compliant with the European Convention for the Protection of Human Rights and Fundamental Freedoms 1950 (ECHR). In particular, the fact that magistrates need to provide 'reasons' for making the order, the availability of the section 48 provision to vary or discharge an order, and the appointment of a guardian would ensure that this would balance the right of a parent to a fair trial, against the need of the child to be protected in an emergency. Where an order is made without notice, the parent/s must be given a full record of the proceedings as soon as possible after the order has taken effect (and see para 5.4.3).

Cases such as *PC and S v UK* [2002] 2 FLR 631 and *Re X (Emergency Protection Orders)* [2006] EWHC 510 (Fam), [2006] 2 FLR 701 should be considered, whereby McFarlane J stressed that an emergency protection order is a draconian and extremely harsh measure, requiring exceptional justification and extraordinarily compelling reasons. One needs to establish 'imminent danger'. Also, the order should be made for no longer than is absolutely necessary in order to protect the child. When an order is made, the local authority is authorised to remove the child only if this is still the proportionate action protect him or her.

Normally, an application to protect a child cannot be made until the child is born. However, there are limited exceptions, such as the one set out in the case of *Bury MBC v D* [2009] EWHC 446 (Fam), [2009] Fam Law 483.

6 Child Assessment Orders

6.1 Effects of order

Child assessment orders were created by section 43 of the Children Act 1989 (CA 1989). They enable the local authority to discover sufficient information about the child to plan appropriate action in the child's interests. *The Children Act 1989 Guidance and Regulations* (DCSF) (*Guidance and Regulations*), Volume 1 *Court Orders*, paragraph 4.12, suggests that a child assessment order application might usefully follow a section 47 investigation, and that this order might be appropriate 'where the harm to the child is long term and cumulative rather than sudden and severe'. It is appropriate where there is no evidence of an emergency situation necessitating immediate removal of a child from home for protection, but the parents or carers of the child are demonstrably failing to co-operate with the local authority in facilitating an assessment. The order can stipulate the nature of the assessment sought, the venue and duration, the person(s) to whom the results are to be given, and the contact between the child and others during the subsistence of the order.

In practice, it has been found that child assessment orders are rarely made, probably because in a situation where parents do not co-operate when the local authority has concerns about a child's welfare, an application for a care order may prove necessary.

Working Together to Safeguard Children: A guide to inter-agency working to safeguard and promote the welfare of children (DCSF, 2010), paragraph 5.70 states that the local authority children's social care department should make all reasonable efforts to persuade parents to co-operate with enquiries under section 47 of the CA 1989.

6.2 Grounds for application

The court may, by section 43(1) of the CA 1989, make the order only if it is satisfied that:

- the applicant has reasonable cause to suspect that the child is suffering, or is likely to suffer, significant harm;

an assessment of the child's state of health or development, or of the way in which he is being treated, is required to enable the applicant to determine whether or not the child is suffering or is likely to suffer significant harm; and

- it is unlikely that such an assessment will be made, or be satisfactory, in the absence of an order under this section.

6.3 Practice and procedure

6.3.1 Application

Application can only be made by a local authority or authorised officer (this category currently only includes the NSPCC), see sections 43(1) and (13) and 31(9) of the CA 1989. Application should be on form C1 together with form C16. It must be determined at a full court hearing. Under section 91(15), no further applications may be made without leave in a six-month period following disposal of the first application.

6.3.2 Venue

Under Article 5(2)(h) of the Allocation and Transfer of Proceedings Order 2008, SI 2008/28, the application should be made in the family proceedings court (FPC) unless there are pending proceedings in the county court or High Court, or they arise out of the same circumstances as gave rise to those proceedings.

6.3.3 Respondents

Notice plus a copy of the application with the date, time and place of hearing, must be served on those listed below who are automatically regarded as respondents to the application.

These include:

(a)   everyone with parental responsibility for the child;

(b)   the child, if of sufficient age and understanding;

(c)   where there is a care order, everyone with parental responsibility before the making of the care order. See rule 12.3 of the FPR 2010.

Others may be joined as respondents, and automatic respondents may be removed by order of the court, rule 12.3(3)(a)–(b) of the FPR 2010.

6.3.4 Notice

Notice of the proceedings on form C6A and the date, time and venue of the application must be given to those entitled, including:

(a) parents;

(b) those with parental responsibility for the child;

(c) any person caring for the child or with whom the child is living;

(d) anyone entitled to contact with the child under a contact order under section 8 or section 34 of the CA 1989;

(e) a local authority providing accommodation for the child;

(f) a person providing a refuge in which the child lives under section 51(1) or (2);

(g) the child, if of sufficient age and understanding.

See section 43(11) of the CA 1989, and rule 12.3 of the FPR 2010 and the accompanying PD 12C, paragraph 3.1.

6.3.5 Service

Service must be at least three days before the directions or application hearing, PD 12 C, paragraph 2.1 accompanying the FPR 2010.

6.3.6 Generally

The principles in section 1 of the CA 1989 apply to section 43 applications, save that the welfare checklist does not apply.

Section 8(3)–(4) of the CA 1989 defines 'family proceedings', and within these proceedings the court has power to make other orders of its own initiative. Section 43 orders are not 'family proceedings'. This means that the court can only make or refuse the order sought, or treat the application as one for an emergency protection order instead, section 43(3). The court must not make a child assessment order if in all the circumstances of the case the court considers an emergency protection order more appropriate, section 43(4).

The duration of the order is limited to seven days from the date specified for commencement, section 43(5) of the CA 1989. The CA 1989 does not state that the seven days must be consecutive, but there seems no other practicable interpretation. It cannot be extended and, unless the court grants permission, it cannot be renewed until a six-month period has elapsed, section 91(15).

6.3.7 Discharge of order

On an application for discharge of a child assessment order, the case will be listed for directions. The procedure is the same as an application for an original order.

6.4 Contact, accommodation and the rights of the child

6.4.1 Contact

If the child is going to be kept away from the family home, then the order shall contain such directions as the court thinks fit in relation to the contact that the child must be allowed to have with other people whilst away from the home, section 43(10) of the CA 1989. Also, it is suggested that the comments in *The Care of Children, Principles and Practice in Regulations and Guidance* (DoH, 1991), paragraphs 14–16 and *Guidance and Regulations*, Volume 4 *Residential Care*, paragraphs 2.5–2.6 are relevant here so that the child should be allowed reasonable contact with:

(a)   parents;

(b)   those with parental responsibility for the child;

(c)   anyone with whom the child was living before the order;

(d)   anyone with a contact order under section 8 or section 34 in force in respect of the child, or anyone acting on the child's behalf;

(e)   anyone with an order for access to the child, section 44(13).

Note the operation of Article 8 of the European Convention for the Protection of Human Rights and Fundamental Freedoms 1950 (ECHR) (right to respect for privacy and family life) as it may affect a child's right to contact with family and siblings.

6.4.2 Accommodation

If the child is removed from the family home and accommodated by the local authority, it is submitted that this would be pursuant to section 20(4) of the CA 1989. In relation to looked after children, the local authority needs to ensure that the placement of the child is in accordance with the Care Planning, Placement and Case Review (England) Regulations 2010, SI 2010/959, applicable as from 1 April 2011.

These regulations were made under the provisions which came under the CA 1989, notably sections 22(c), 23(za), 23(zb), 25A and 25B, as well as Schedule 2, paragraphs 12(a)–(e), brought in by the Children and Young Persons Act 2008.

One of the key provisions under the CA 1989 is that, pursuant to section 22(4) of the CA 1989, in determining the child's placement, the local authority needs to, in so far as is reasonably practicable, ascertain the views of, amongst others, the child (if of sufficient age and understanding) and the child's parents.

6.4.3 Rights of the child

A child of sufficient age and understanding has the right to be consulted and informed about events that are happening, see *Guidance and Regulations*, Volume 4 *Residential Care*, paragraphs 2.20(c), 2.21 and 2.10–2.12.

The child assessment order will usually include a direction about medical or psychiatric assessment of the child. Examinations can be ordered or prohibited. Directions can include venue, personnel to be present and nomination of the person(s) to whom results of assessments, etc. should be given. A child of sufficient age and understanding has the right to make an informed refusal of medical or psychiatric assessment, section 43(8) of the CA 1989. A '*Gillick*-competent' child, or a young person over 16, may consent to or refuse medical treatment. See Chapter 12.

A child should only be kept away from home where it is absolutely necessary for assessment purposes, and in accordance with directions in the order, section 43(9)(b) and (c) of the CA 1989.

6.5 Appeals, variation and discharge

Appeal lies against the making or refusal of a child assessment order, from the FPC to the High Court and from the county court or High Court to the Court of Appeal.

Applications to vary or discharge the order (under section 43(12) of the CA 1989) may be made on form C1, with two days' notice, to the court which made the original order. See PD 12C, paragraphs 1.1 and 2.1 accompanying the FPR 2010.

Contraventions of the ECHR may be dealt with by complaint, judicial review or appeal against a court order.

7 Care and Supervision Proceedings

7.1 Care order – definitions

'Care orders' are those orders made under section 31 of the CA 1989 placing a child into the care of a designated local authority. The 'designated local authority' is the local authority for the area in which the child resides, or within whose area any circumstances arose in consequence of which the care order is being made.

A 'child' is a person under the age of 18, section 105(1) of the CA 1989. The term care order includes an 'interim care order' made under section 38 as well as an order made under section 31. Reference to a 'child in the care of the local authority' is defined by section 105(1) to mean a child subject to a care order (and not therefore a child who is accommodated by a local authority under a section 20 voluntary care arrangement), although children who are in the care of the local authority are also 'looked after' and the same planning and review regime applies as for accommodated children).

7.2 Grounds for application for a care or supervision order

A care order cannot be made in respect of a child over 17 years old, or 16 if married, section 31(3) of the CA 1989.

Under the CA 1989 there is only one route into statutory care. The court must be satisfied that the criteria set out in section 31 are met and also that an order is necessary for the welfare of the child.

The underlying principles in section 1(1), (2) and (5) of the CA 1989 – the paramountcy of the welfare of the child, avoidance of delay and no order unless necessary – all apply. The court must have regard to the welfare checklist in section 1(3), see Chapter 2.

Care orders and supervision orders are mutually exclusive, but the grounds in section 31 for the application for both are the same. On hearing an application for a care order, if the threshold criteria are met, the court may instead order supervision, or vice versa. Where a rder is in force, the court may, at any time during it, substitute rvision, but the making of the supervision order will discharge the existing care order.

Section 31(1) of the CA 1989 specifies the grounds for application for a care or supervision order:

(a) that the child concerned is suffering, or likely to suffer, significant harm; and

(b) that the harm; or likelihood of harm, is attributable to:

(i) the care given to the child, or likely to be given to him if an order were not made, not being what it would be reasonable to expect a parent to give to him; or

(ii) the child's being beyond parental control.

The following definitions are taken from section 31(9) of the CA 1989.

Development

Physical, intellectual, emotional, social or behavioural development.

Harm

Ill treatment or the impairment of health or development, including, for example, impairment suffered from seeing or hearing the ill-treatment of another.

Health

Includes physical or mental health.

Ill treatment

Includes sexual abuse and forms of ill treatment which are not physical.

7.3 Significant harm

The difficult part for practitioners in care and supervision proceedings is often the definition and proof of 'significant harm'. Section 31(9) of the CA 1989 gives the definitions (see above). It is also provided in section 31(10) that: 'Where the question of whether harm suffered by a child is significant turns upon the child's health or development, his health or development shall be compared with that which could reasonably be expected of a similar child'. The court will therefore have to compare this particular child with a notional similar child, of similar background, age, ethnicity, culture, race, religion and physique. See Figure 3.

Figure 3   Significant harm flowchart

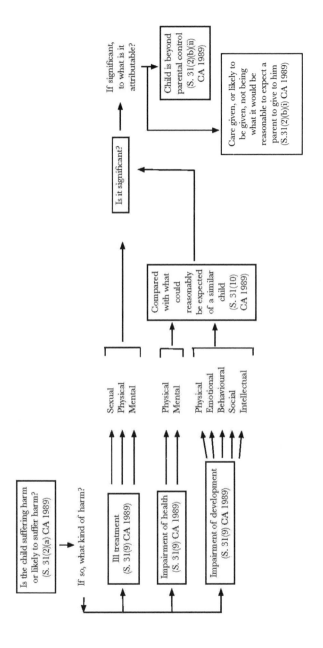

Significant harm must be attributable to parental care falling below a reasonable standard, or the child being beyond parental control. The test is objective, measured against a reasonable standard of parenting. It was suggested in *Humberside CC v B* [1993] 1 FLR 257 that 'significant' means 'considerable, noteworthy or important'. However, the definition became problematic in *Re MA (Care Threshold)* [2009] EWCA Civ 853.

In *Re M (Minor) (Care Order: Threshold Conditions)* [1994] 2 AC 424, [1994] 3 WLR 558, the House of Lords held that 'is suffering' means at the date of the hearing, or at the moment when the child protection was initiated, provided that the protection is uninterrupted until the date of the hearing. A careful reading of this judgment is recommended. Whilst the court may find the grounds proved, it may also take account of the circumstances prevailing at the hearing date in considering whether it is necessary to make an order, and which order would be most appropriate.

7.3.1   Standard of proof

The threshold criteria for proceedings under section 31 of the CA 1989 must be established on a 'simple balance of probabilities', i.e. significant harm (unlike the 'likelihood' element mentioned at 7.2) must be established on a balance of probabilities. The House of Lords put it very clearly as '... a real possibility, a possibility that cannot be sensibly ignored, having regard to the nature and gravity of the feared harm in the particular case ...'. See *Re H and Others (Child Sexual Abuse: Standard of Proof)* [1996] 1 All ER 1, [1996] 1 FLR 80, a section 31 application in respect of four children based on an allegation that the father had sexually abused the oldest child, and positing a likelihood of significant harm to the younger three. The court found that the section 31(2) criteria were not met in the case of the oldest child, leaving no power to go on and even consider the likelihood of harm to the younger three children.

Difficulties in reaching the standard of proof occurred in subsequent cases because of dicta in *Re H and Others* (above) suggesting that the more serious the allegation, the greater the level of proof needed. However, in *Re B (Children) (Sexual abuse: Standard of proof)* [2008] UKHL 35, [2008] 2 FCR 339, Baroness Hale clarified that the standard of proof necessary to establish threshold under section 31 is the 'simple balance of probabilities, nothing more nor less'.

Under section 31 of the CA 1989, the local authority must also prove that the harm was attributable to the parents' care (or lack of care). This can cause difficulties in the case of 'uncertain perpetrators' when it is not known which parent or carer was responsible for an injury. In *Re O and N (Children) (Non-accidental injury)* [2003] UKHL 18, the House of Lords held that where an injury could be attributed to the parents but neither would say who was responsible, the court should proceed to the welfare stage on the basis that each is a possible perpetrator.

7.4 Practice and procedure

7.4.1 Applicants

Only a local authority or authorised person may apply for a care order, section 31(1) of the CA 1989. An 'authorised person' at the moment is an officer of the NSPCC, section 31(9), although we could find no record of the NSPCC using this provision.

The court has no power to make a care order without an application, but under section 38(1) of the CA 1989 it may make an interim care or supervision order on adjourning an application for a full order; or alongside making a direction to the local authority to investigate the child's circumstances under section 37.

Under rule 29.4 of the Family Procedure Rules 2010, SI 2010/2955 (FPR 2010), any application relating to care proceedings cannot be withdrawn without the permission of the court.

7.4.2 Venue

Applications should be made in the family proceedings court (FPC), unless one of three exceptions apply: there has been a court-directed investigation under section 37 of the CA 1989; there are pending proceedings; or the application is to extend, vary or discharge an existing order in a higher court. In these exceptional cases, the application may be made in the same court as the other proceedings, Allocation and Transfer of Proceedings Order 2008, SI 2008/28.

There are several classes of county courts in family proceedings: divorce centres, care centres, family hearing centres, adoption centres, intercountry adoption centres and forced marriage county courts (Article 2 of the Allocation and Transfer of Proceedings Order 2008). Care and supervision applications must be heard in care centres.

It may be appropriate for a care or supervision application to be heard in a higher court. Transfers are governed by the Allocation and Transfer of Proceedings Order 2008, supplemented by the *Practice Direction (Allocation and Transfer of Proceedings)* of 3 November 2008. Here there is space only to summarise these provisions, and to draw attention to potential pitfalls which may be encountered. If the procedural requirements are broken, proceedings are not invalidated (Article 4 of the Allocation and Transfer of Proceedings Order 2008).

Cases may only be started or transferred up to the High Court if they are exceptionally complex, the outcome is important to the general public, or there is another substantial reason (Articles 7 and 18 of the Allocation and Transfer of Proceedings Order 2008).

7.4.3 Form

Application must be made on form C1 (or form C2 if made in existing proceedings) with forms C6 and C110 and the Annex Documents listed in the pre-proceedings checklist in PD 12A accompanying the FPR 2010. These are the social work chronology, the initial social work statement, the initial and core assessments, the letter/s before proceedings, the schedule of proposed findings and the care plan.

7.4.4 Respondents

Notice of proceedings with date and place of hearing, together with a copy of the application endorsed with the date of the hearing or directions, must be served three days before the hearing on those listed below who are automatically considered respondents to the application:

(a)   everyone who the local authority believes has parental responsibility for the child;

(b)   the child, if of sufficient age and understanding.

See rule 12.3 of the FPR 2010 regarding parties, and Part 6 regarding service. Others may be joined as respondents and automatic respondents may be removed by direction of the court. Under rule 12.3(2) any person who has parental responsibility who has not already been made a respondent will be joined by the court on that person's request.

7.4.5 Notice and court actions on issue

When the proceedings are issued, the court will consider allocation of the case and the appropriate level of court. It will also set a date for the first appointment and notify the parties of the date, time and venue of the application. This is discussed in para 7.7.

Under PD 12C accompanying the FPR 2010, notice must be given to any of the following non-parties on form 6A:

- a local authority looking after the child;
- a person caring for the child when the proceedings commence;
- if the child is staying in a refuge, the provider of that refuge service;
- every person the applicant believes to be a party in pending relevant proceedings;
- every person who the applicant believes to be a parent of the child who does not have parental responsibility.

7.4.6 Service

Part 6 of the FPR 2010 and the accompanying PD 6A deal with service of documents on respondents. The court can dispense with the requirements of service under rule 6.36.

7.4.7 Attendance

Proceedings may take place in the child's absence if the court considers this in his interests, having regard to the matters to be discussed or the evidence likely to be given, and he is represented by a solicitor, rule 12.14(3) of the FPR 2010.

The other parties and/or their legal representatives have to attend directions appointments and hearings unless otherwise directed by the court. If respondents fail to appear, the court may proceed in their absence. If applicants fail to attend, the court may refuse their application, rule 12.14(5)–(7) of the FPR 2010. For discussion of case preparation, see Chapter 12.

7.5 Interim orders

On adjourning a care or supervision application, the court has the power to make an interim order when satisfied that there are reasonable grounds for believing the circumstances justifying a care order exist, section 38(2) of the CA 1989. An interim order's maximum duration is an initial maximum of eight weeks, followed by extensions of up to four weeks each. Shorter interim orders are possible, section 38(4) and (5):

(a)   the initial interim order may be up to eight weeks;

(b)   if the initial order is less than eight weeks, then the second interim order must be no more than a total of eight weeks less the duration of the initial interim order (for example, first order five weeks, second order three weeks; or first order two weeks, second six);

(c)   any subsequent orders must be of no more than four weeks' duration.

On making an interim order, directions may require medical or psychiatric examination or assessment of the child, which a child of sufficient understanding may refuse, section 38(6) of the CA 1989. (See Chapter 12 for the rights of children.) Directions may prevent the abuse of children by repeated examinations, section 38(7). Directions may also govern the time and venue of the examination, who shall be present and to whom the results will be given.

Directions for assessment under section 38 of the CA 1989 can include assessments of the parents' capacity, for example, as part of a residential parent and child assessment (*Re C (A Minor) (Interim Care order) (Residential Assessment)* [1997] AC 489) but not to provide treatment or therapy for parents (*Re G (A Minor) (Interim Care order) (Residential Assessments)* [2005] UKHL 68).

7.6   Effects of care order

7.6.1   Duration

A care order subsists until the child reaches 18, unless brought to an end earlier by the court, section 91(1) and (12) of the CA 1989.

A care order will cease on the making of:

(a)   an adoption order under section 46(2)(b) of the Adoption and Children Act 2002;

(b)   a placement order made under section 29(1) of the Adoption and Children Act 2002 (a care order will not take effect whilst this order is in force);

(c)   a special guardianship order section 91(5)(a) of the CA 1989;

(d)   a residence order, section 91(1) of the CA 1989;

(e)   a supervision order made in substitution for a care order, section 39(4) of the CA 1989;

(f)   an order for discharge of care, section 39(1) of the CA 1989.

A care order will also cease:

(g)   when a child goes to live in Northern Ireland, the Isle of Man or the Channel Islands, provided the relevant regulations are satisfied, section 101(4) of the CA 1989 (it should be noted that the regulations about this have not yet been made under section 101(4)).

7.6.2   Parental responsibility and care plans

The local authority acquires parental responsibility under a care order, sharing it with those who already have it. The local authority may, however, limit the exercise of parental responsibility by others whilst the care order subsists, section 33(3) of the CA 1989. There are limits on the powers of the local authority during a care order. The local authority may not change a child's religion, consent to his adoption or appoint a guardian for the child, section 33. The parental responsibility which others had when the care order was made still subsists, but it cannot be exercised in a way which conflicts with a court order, section 2(6) and (8). The child's name may not be changed or the child removed from the UK without written consent of all with parental responsibility or leave of the court, section 33(7).

The local authority may remove the child from the jurisdiction of the court for up to one month and, under Schedule 2, paragraph 19 to the CA 1989, can make arrangements for a child to live abroad, with certain restrictions. For care plans, see LAC (99)29 and NAFWC 1/2000 in Wales. See the House of Lords' decision in *Re S (Minors) (Care Order: Implementation of Care Plan), Re W (Minors) (Care Order: Adequacy of Care Plan)* [2002] UKHL 10, [2002] 1 FLR 815. The local authority must provide a care plan when applying for a care order, section 31A(2), and keep it under review. After the care order is made, the court has limited powers to intervene.

7.6.3   Proportionality, kinship care and local authority accommodation of the child

Hale LJ expressed the purpose of the CA 1989 as follows, 'The principle has to be that the local authority works to support, and eventually reunite, the family, unless the risks are so high that the child's welfare requires alternative family care', *Re C and B (Care Order: Future Harm)*[2001] 1 FLR 611.

Proportionality is therefore vital to comply with Article 8 of the European Convention for the Protection of Human Rights and Fundamental Freedoms 1950 (ECHR). *The Children Act 1989 Guidance and Regulations* (DCSF) (*Guidance and Regulations*), Volume 2 *Care Planning, Placement and Case Review* governs the placements of children in residential and foster care and placements with their immediate family or in the 'kinship care' of wider family and friends.

The guidance emphasises the duty on the local authority to keep children with their birth family if at all possible, consistent with their welfare, and the importance of maintaining family links and of the primary duty to try to keep children with their family by the provision of resources.

If the child needs to live away from home, then under section 33(1) of the CA 1989, the local authority has a duty to receive the child into its care once the order is made. The child is the responsibility of the local authority, and it must provide for somewhere to live and maintenance for the child, section 23(1).

During the period the child is subject to an interim care order (section 38 of the CA 1989) or care order (section 31), he or she is looked after by the local authority and therefore subject to the same planning and review regime in the *Guidance and Regulations* as children accommodated voluntarily under section 20. *Guidance and Regulations*, Volume 3 *Family Placements* sets out the local authority's duties to assist the young person in care in transition into adulthood.

7.6.4   Contact with a child in care

Guidance and Regulations, Volume 2 *Care Planning, Placement and Case Review*, paragraphs 2.87–2.92 set out the section 34 presumption that contact with his or her family is in the best interests of a child in care unless proved otherwise. Parents and others in financial or practical difficulty should receive help with travelling to contact sessions, Schedule 2, paragraph 16 to the CA 1989.

Contact with children in care is subject to the control of the court, if it cannot be agreed between the parents (or other persons with parental responsibility) and the local authority. This is different from contact in private law, where there is no legal presumption for or against contact.

The CA 1989 requires that children looked after by a local authority under a care order will be afforded 'reasonable contact' with those people listed in section 34(1). They are:

(a)   parents;

(b)   guardians;

(c)   anyone with a residence order in force immediately before the care order was made;

(d)   anyone with care of the child under a High Court order made under its inherent jurisdiction.

The court may, on the application of the children's guardian or the child, make whatever order it considers appropriate in respect of contact between the child and any named person. Where the child or the local authority is the applicant, the scope of the order is very wide. On the application of any person entitled to contact under section 34(1) of the CA 1989 (those listed above), or anyone else with leave of the court, a contact order may be made.

When the court makes a care order, it may make a contact order if necessary in the interests of the child, section 34(5) of the CA 1989. The forms, those entitled to notice and respondents, are the same as for the care order.

In urgent cases, if necessary, a local authority may stop contact for up to seven days, section 34(6) of the CA 1989. If it wishes to stop contact for longer, it must apply to the court for a care contact order under section 34, authorising contact with a named person to be curtailed or to be refused. It is argued that severe curtailment of contact is tantamount to a refusal within the meaning of section 34 since the section refers to 'reasonable contact' and the court is the ultimate arbiter of reasonableness. In *Re B (Minors) (Termination of Contact: Paramount Consideration)* [1993] Fam 301 at 311, Butler-Sloss LJ stated that contact must not be allowed to destabilise or endanger the arrangements for the child and that in many cases the local authority's plan will be decisive. She described the task of the court as having 'the greatest respect' for the local authority's plans to arrange contact in the best interests of the child, but also retaining the power to adjudicate these arrangements if they are not agreed between the local authority and those named in section 34(1).

Contact between looked after children and their parents and significant others, during care proceedings and beyond, is a fundamental component of proceedings and is often the cause of most conflict between the parties as to the right level and provision.

Within care proceedings, contact is invariably supervised by the local authority or its agent. The focus of the supervision is to ensure the safety of the child, protect him or her from being drawn into the court process by parents or visiting relatives, and to allow for regular observations of adult and child interactions, which feeds into the court process and the assessments of parenting and arrangements for future contact.

Within care proceedings the level of contact provided should not be pre-emptive of the final hearing, and should ensure that it is maintained at a sufficient level to keep the doors open to future reunification. Young babies will receive the highest levels of contact with birth parents, particularly where there is a possibility of reunification, placement in a residential assessment facility or a mother and baby foster placement.

There are occasions when it becomes evident that the quality of the contact and of the parent/child interactions are so poor that a reduction needs to be made before the conclusion of the proceedings in order to safeguard the welfare of the child. Such decisions are invariably contentious and often lead to contested interim hearings.

There are occasions when it may become necessary for the local authority to suspend contact under section 34(6) of the CA 1989, for example if a child is harmed, abducted, or threatened with abduction, if there is violent behaviour or parents attending heavily under the influence of drugs or alcohol. The local authority can suspend contact for seven days before the matter needs to return to court for adjudication.

Care plans should detail the future proposals for contact and they require careful scrutiny, particularly by the child's legal representative and the children's guardian. The arrangements for contact at a final hearing often cause much greater conflict than the making of the care order and a recognition that a child will not return to the care of his or her parent(s). Contact is a complex area and the children's guardian is best placed to advise on the current and future arrangements.

7.6.5 Rights of the child in care proceedings and under a care order

A child who is subject to an interim care order under section 38 of the CA 1989 or to a care order under section 31 has rights which are protected by the Human Rights Act 1998, the CA 1989 and also by the guidance issued under it. The child has a right to:

(a) refuse medical or psychiatric assessment ordered within an interim care order under section 38(6) of the CA 1989;

(b) contact with his or her family (see para 7.6.4), and see *Guidance and Regulations*, Volume 2, paragraphs 2.78–2.93;

(c) consultation: before making any decision with respect to a child being looked after by the local authority, the court must, so far as reasonably practicable, ascertain the wishes and feelings of the child, and give them due consideration, having regard to the child's age and understanding, see *Guidance and Regulations*, Volume 2, paragraphs 1.9–1.13 and section 22(4) and (5) of the CA 1989;

(d) participate in the care planning process, see section 22(4) of the CA 1989 and regulation 5a of the Care Planning, Placement and Case Review Regulations 2010, SI 2010/959 (the 2010

Regulations). This includes the permanence plan, health plan and personal education plan (PEP);

(e)   a review of the plan within 20 days of becoming looked after, then within three months and then every six months, see regulation 33 of the 2010 Regulations;

(f)   be allocated a named independent reviewing officer (IRO) who the child will meet before each review. The IRO's role is set out in detail in the *IRO Handbook: Statutory guidance for independent reviewing officers and local authorities on their functions in relation to case management and review for looked after children* (DfE, 2010) which accompanies *Guidance and Regulations*, Volume 2;

(g)   be advised by the IRO, in accordance with the child's age and understanding, of his or her rights to make court applications or complaints and access to advocacy services and legal advice, regulation 45 of the 2010 Regulations and *Guidance and Regulations*, Volume 2, paragraphs 2.102–2.104;

(h)   an independent visitor, regulations 28–31 of the 2010 Regulations and *Guidance and Regulations*, Volume 2, paragraphs 3.155–3.158 and 3.184–3.212;

(i)   services to assist young people in the transition into adulthood. These are not covered in this book but are found in sections inserted into the CA 1989 by the Children (Leaving Care) Act 2000 (Schedule 2, paragraph 19; sections 23(a)–(E) and 24) and in detail in *Guidance and Regulations*, Volume 3.

7.6.6   Rights of parents of a child in care

Parents (with parental responsibility or not) and those with parental responsibility for a child in care, have the right to:

(a)   consultation and participation, section 22(4) of the CA 1989 and the 2010 Regulations;

(b)   information on where their child is being kept, Schedule 2, paragraph 15(2) to the CA 1989;

(c)   reasonable contact with their child, section 34 of the CA 1989;

(d)   receive financial or practical assistance with travelling to see their child, Schedule 2, paragraph 16 to the CA 1989.

If the local authority departs from the care plan in breach of the child's ECHR rights, under sections 7 and 8 of the Human Rights Act 1998 the court may grant relief or remedy.

7.7   *Public Law Outline* – principles, 'split hearings', issues resolution, interim and final hearings

7.7.1   Main principles of the *Public Law Outline*

Under PD 12A accompanying the FPR 2010, the main principles underlying court case management in public law proceedings are:

(1)   timetable for the child: see paragraphs 3.2–3.9;

(2)   judicial continuity: each case will be allocated to one or two case management judges or case managers, who will be responsible for every case management stage through to the final hearing and, in relation to the High Court or county court, one of whom may be – and where possible should be – the judge who will conduct the final hearing;

(3)   main case management tools: each case will be managed by the court by using the appropriate main case management tools;

(4)   active case management: each case will be actively case managed by the court with a view at all times to furthering the overriding objective;

(5)   consistency: each case will, so far as compatible with the overriding objective, be managed in a consistent way and using the standardised steps.

The main case management tools are:

•   *The timetable for the child* who is the subject of the proceedings. Setting out all significant steps in the child's life that are likely to take place during the proceedings, to include legal, health care, social care, review and other steps.

See rule 8 of the FPR 2010, which inserts a definition of the timetable for the child in rule 4.14A of the FPR 1991:

> 4.14A.—(1) In proceedings for a care order or a supervision order, the court shall set the timetable of the proceedings in accordance with the Timetable for the Child.
>
> (2) The "Timetable for the Child" means the timetable set by the court in accordance with its duties under sections 1 and 32 of the Act of 1989 and shall—
>
> > (a) take into account dates of the significant steps in the life of the child who is the subject of the proceedings; and
> >
> > (b) be appropriate for that child.

- *Case management documentation* which, under paragraph 3.10 includes:
  - application form and annexed documents;
  - case analysis and recommendations provided by CAFCASS or CAFCASS Cymru;
  - local authority case summary;
  - other parties' case summaries.
- *Case management record* under paragraph 3.12. This is the court's filing system under the PLO and will include:
  - case management documentation;
  - standard directions on issue and on first appointment;
  - case management orders approved by the court.

7.7.2 Four stages of the *Public Law Outline*

- Stage 1 – Issue of application, allocation record, and pre-proceedings checklist and first appointment.
- Stage 2 – Advocates meeting, draft case management order, and case management conference.
- Stage 3 – Advocates meeting, draft case management order, issues resolution hearing.
- Stage 4 – Final hearing and directions.

Often, cases present issues of fact which require identification, clarification or determination. The intention is that these should be narrowed to those still outstanding at the issues resolution hearing (IRH) stage by the use of directions at the case management conference (CMC) stage. Cases may be resolved at the IRH stage, thus dispensing with the need for a final hearing.

7.7.3 Split hearings

Before the PLO came into force, the term 'split hearings' (meaning the separate hearings in which the process of fact finding, threshold criteria and subsequent disposal were decided in stages) was commonly used. 'Fact finding' hearings are used to clarify and adjudicate on factual matters in dispute, for example identification of the perpetrator in cases of sexual or physical abuse, and are split off from the final hearing of the case. Guidance has been given in a plethora of case law on the use of split hearings, for example in *Re P (Care Proceedings: Split Hearing)* [2007] EWCA Civ 1265, [2008] Fam Law 202 and *Re A*

(Children) (Split Hearings: Practice) [2006] EWCA Civ 714. The *President's Guidance in Relation to Split Hearings* [2010] 2 FCR 271 cautions against holding a separate threshold or fact-finding hearing unless the court cannot proceed without this.

7.7.4 *Public Law Outline* checklists

Pre-proceedings checklist

For a detailed and authoritative explanation of the PLO, see P Pressdee et al, *The Public Law Outline: The Court Companion* (Family Law, 2008), and also see *Best Practice Guide – Preparing for Care and Supervision Proceedings* (Ministry of Justice, 2009).

Annex documents to be attached to the application form:

- social work chronology;
- initial social work statement;
- initial and core assessments;
- letters before proceedings;
- schedule of proposed findings;
- care plan.

Documents to be disclosed from the local authority's files, normally by the day before the first appointment:

- previous court orders and judgments/reasons;
- any relevant assessment materials:
  - section 7 and section 37 reports;
  - relatives and friends materials (e.g. a genogram);
- other relevant reports and records:
  - single, joint or inter-agency materials (e.g. health and education/Home Office and immigration documents);
  - records of discussions with the family;
  - key local authority minutes and records for the child (including strategy discussion record);
- pre-existing care plans (e.g. child in need plan, looked after child plan and child protection plan).

Stage 1 Issue and the first appointment

Objectives: to ensure compliance with pre-proceedings checklist; to allocate proceedings; to obtain the information necessary for initial case management at the first appointment.

On day one:

- local authority files:
    - application form and annex documents
- court officer issues application;
- court nominates case manager(s);
- court gives standard directions on issue including:
    - pre-proceedings checklist compliance
    - allocate and/or transfer
    - appoint children's guardian
    - appoint solicitor for the child
    - case analysis for first appointment
    - invite Official Solicitor to act for protected persons (non subject children and incapacitated adults)
    - list first appointment by day six
    - make arrangements for contested hearing (if necessary)

By day three:

- allocation of a children's guardian expected;
- local authority serves the application form and annex documents on parties;
- parties notify local authority and court of need for a contested hearing;
- court makes arrangements for a contested hearing;
- initial case management by court including:
    - confirm timetable for the child
    - confirm allocation or transfer
    - identify additional parties and representation (including allocation of children's guardian)
    - identify 'early final hearing' cases
    - scrutinise care plan

- court gives standard directions on first appointment including:
  - case analysis and recommendations for Stages 2 and 3
  - preparation and service of any missing documents
  - local authority case summary
  - other parties' case summaries
  - parties' initial witness statements
  - for the advocates' meeting
  - list case management conference or (if appropriate) an early final hearing
  - upon transfer

Stage 2 Case management conference

Advocates' meeting – no later than two days before case management conference.

Objectives: to prepare the draft case management order; to identify experts and draft questions for them.

Tasks:

- consider all other parties' case summaries and case analysis and recommendations;
- identify proposed experts and draft questions in accordance with experts practice direction;
- draft case management order;
- notify court of need for a contested hearing;
- file draft case management order with the case manager/case management judge by 11am one working day before the case management conference.

Case management conference – no later than day 45.

Objectives: to identify issue(s); to give full case management directions.

Tasks:

- detailed case management by the court:
  - scrutinise compliance with directions
  - review and confirm timetable for the child
  - identify key issue(s)

—   confirm allocation or transfer

– consider case management directions in the draft case management order

– scrutinise care plan

– check compliance with experts practice direction

- court issues case management order;

- court lists IRH and, where necessary, a warned period for final hearing.

Stage 3 Issues resolution hearing

Advocates' meeting – between two and seven days before the issues resolution hearing.

Objective: to prepare or update the draft case management order.

Tasks:

- consider all other parties' case summaries and case analysis and recommendations;

- draft case management order;

- notify court of need for a contested hearing/time for oral evidence to be given;

- file draft case management order with the case manager/case management judge by 11am one working day before the IRH.

Issues resolution hearing – between 16 and 25 weeks.

Objectives: to resolve and narrow issue(s); to identify any remaining key issues.

Tasks:

- identification by the court of the key issue(s) (if any) to be determined;

- final case management by the court:

– scrutinise compliance with directions

– consider case management directions in the draft case management order

– scrutinise care plan;

– give directions for hearing documents;

- threshold agreement or facts/issues remaining to be determined

- final evidence and care plan

- case analysis and recommendations

- witness templates

- skeleton arguments

- judicial reading list/reading time/judgment writing time

- time estimate

- bundles practice direction compliance

- list or confirm hearing

• court issues case management order

Stage 4 Hearing

Hearing set in accordance with the timetable for the child.

Objective: to determine remaining issues.

• all file and serve updated case management documents and bundle;

• draft final order(s) in approved form;

• judgment/reasons;

• disclose documents as required after hearing.

7.8   Assessments and care planning

Only when the threshold grounds (criteria in s 31 of the CA 1989) are established, will the court go on to consider what, if any, order to make.

No care order may be made unless the court has first considered a care plan submitted by the local authority, section 31(3A) of the CA 1989 and see LAC 99(29).

The next task for the court, therefore, once the criteria in section 31 of the CA 1989 are satisfied, is to consider the circumstances of the child in the context of the underlying principles of the CA 1989, to consider the welfare checklist, to decide whether the making of an order is necessary in the best interests of the child and, if so, which order would be the most appropriate in all the circumstances of the case.

The courts subject care plans to very careful scrutiny. Evidence should be called in support of care plans, and known placement details made available to the court. Note that, once the care order is made the court can no longer control events. In *Re S (Minors) (Care Order: Implementation of Care Plan), Re W (Minors) (Care Order: Adequacy of Care Plan)* [2002] UKHL 10, [2002] 1 FLR 815, the House of Lords affirmed the right of local authorities to discharge their responsibility under care orders without interference from the courts. However, since this case was heard, the role of the Independent Reporting Office was introduced to protect the interests of the child, section 118 of the Adoption and Children Act 2002, now in section 26 of the CA 1989.

If the grounds are satisfied, much of the court's time will then be spent on considering proportionality, and assessment and discussion of the timetable and care plan, in order to make the best decision for the child's short- and long-term future. However, the *Family Justice Review* (*Family Justice Review Final Report* (Ministry of Justice, 2011)) has identified this as a cause of unnecessary delay and has recommended that courts' scrutiny of care plans be curtailed.

7.9   Effects of supervision order

The grounds for granting a supervision order are the same as for a care order under section 31 of the CA 1989, and will be granted if this is the proportionate order to make. It may initially be applied for, or made by the court when considering the range of its powers under section 1(3)(g).

A supervision order places the child under the supervision of a local authority or a probation officer. The duties and powers of the supervising officer are set out in section 35 of and Schedule 3 to the CA 1989, including a duty 'to advise, assist and befriend' the child. The supervising officer does not acquire parental responsibility for the child. The sanction for failure to co-operate with supervision is an application to discharge the order and to substitute something else, possibly a care order.

Directions may be made within supervision orders binding those responsible for the child and also the child to attend activities or live at specified places (see para 7.9.3). They subsist for the duration of the supervision order or such lesser period as the court may specify

A supervision requirement imposed by a youth rehabilitation order is possible within criminal proceedings on a finding of guilt against a juvenile offender under section 1 of the Criminal Justice and Immigration Act 2008. Under Schedule 1, paragraph 9 of the 2008

Act, 'supervision requirement', in relation to a youth rehabilitation order, means a requirement that, during the period for which the order remains in force, the offender must attend appointments with the responsible officer or another person determined by the responsible officer, at such times and places as the officer decides.

The criteria in section 31 of the CA 1989 do not have to be met before a 'youth rehabilitation order' is made. A criminal court cannot make a care order. Criminal supervision orders are not discussed in this book because they are different from orders made under section 31. However, a child in local authority accommodation or fostering under section 1 and Schedule 1, paragraphs 17–19 of a youth rehabilitation order is 'looked after' and must have the same rights under the 2010 Regulations as a child living away from home under a CA 1989 care or supervision order.

7.9.1 Interim orders

If a care or supervision application is adjourned, the court can make an interim order, section 38(1) of the CA 1989. In the context of interim care or supervision orders, the court can make directions for medical or psychiatric assessment which a child of sufficient age and understanding may refuse, section 38(6) and (7); and the court may also make an exclusion requirement under section 38(A), ordering a named person to leave and/or excluding him or her from entering a dwelling house or defined geographical area in which the child lives. A power of arrest may be attached to the exclusion order, enforceable by the police, section 38(A)(5)–(9), rule 12.28 of the FPR 2010 and the accompanying PD 12K.

Where the court has power to impose an exclusion requirement in an interim care order, undertakings may be accepted from the relevant person, section 38(B) of the CA 1989. However, undertakings, although they are enforceable as an order of the court, cannot be coupled with a power of arrest.

Section 38(3) of the CA 1989 provides that if there is an application for care, but the court decides to make a residence order (for limited duration) instead of a care order, then the court must also make an interim supervision order unless it is satisfied that the child's welfare will be adequately safeguarded without one.

7.9.2 Duration of care and supervision

A supervision order may last for up to one year, section 91(3) of and Schedule 3, paragraph 6 to the CA 1989. It may be for shorter duration if so ordered by the court. A supervision order may also be extended by the court on a subsequent hearing for a further period or periods of up to a year, to a maximum of three years from the date it was first made, Schedule 3, paragraph 6(3) and (4). Section 1 principles apply, see Chapter 2 and *Wakefield MDC UT* [2008] EWCA Civ 199, [2008] Fam Law 485.

7.9.3 Directions in supervision orders

Directions to the child

The court may embody in the order specific requirements with which the child is to comply; and/or a general term along the lines that 'the child must comply with the directions given from time to time by the supervisor'. The supervisor then has a certain amount of leeway about the directions given, provided they fall within the parameters set in Schedule 3, paragraph 2 to the CA 1989.

The parameters are:

(a) to live at a place or places specified;

(b) to present himself to a person or persons specified for a period or periods specified;

(c) to participate in specified activities on dates and at times specified.

Directions to a 'responsible person'

A responsible person is defined in Schedule 3, paragraph 1 to the CA 1989 as 'a person who has parental responsibility for the child, and any other person with whom the child is living'.

Under Schedule 3 to the CA 1989, with the consent of the responsible person, the court can include in the order a number of requirements:

(a) to take reasonable steps to ensure the child complies with the directions of the supervisor under Schedule 3, paragraph 2 (that is, to live at a specified place, present himself to a person specified on a specific day and to participate in activities);

(b) to take all reasonable steps to ensure the supervised child complies with directions regarding medical and psychiatric examinations, Schedule 3, paragraphs 3–5;

(c) that he or she comply with direction of supervisor 'to attend at a place specified in the directions for the purpose of taking part in activities so specified'.

A supervision order may also direct the responsible person to keep the supervisor informed of change of address, and to allow the supervisor to visit the child at the place where they are living.

The responsible person may be directed to ensure the child complies with the supervisor's programme, giving the order a better chance of success. The adult may be asked to attend a treatment centre, to benefit the family and enable the child to remain at home.

The county court has no jurisdiction to accept undertakings in care or supervision cases, *Re B (A Minor) (Supervision Order: Parental Undertaking)* [1996] 1 FLR 676.

The court has no jurisdiction to specify the activities in which the responsible person (with the court's consent) is to participate. This is for the supervisor to arrange. The supervisor can therefore direct a sex offender to have treatment, *Re H (Minors) (Terms of Supervision Orders)* [1994] Fam Law 486.

The court may authorise medical or psychiatric examination, and also direct attendance by the child and/or carers for medical or psychiatric examination of the child, or, if necessary, in-patient or outpatient treatment, which a child of sufficient understanding has a right to refuse (see Chapter 12 and Schedule 3, paragraphs 4 and 5 to the CA 1989). Although the supervisor has the power to direct attendance by the child for medical or psychiatric examination or assessment, only the court can authorise medical or psychological examination. Before making these directions, the court must know that satisfactory arrangements have been, or can be, made for the treatment proposed. This implies that the practitioners concerned have indicated that they agree to carry it out. If the child has sufficient understanding, his or her consent is also required.

If a health practitioner is unwilling to continue treatment of the child, or the directions need altering because of any of the following circumstances:

(a)   the treatment should be extended beyond the period specified in the order;

(b)   different treatment is required;

(c)   the child is not susceptible to treatment; or

(d)   no further treatment is required;

he must submit a written report to the supervisor, who must then put that report back to the court for revision of the directions, Schedule 3, paragraph 5(6)–(7) of the CA 1989.

7.9.4 Enforcement

If there is a direction that the supervisor visits the child, and this is prevented, then the supervisor may bring the matter back to court for a warrant for a police officer to 'assist the supervisor to exercise these powers, using reasonable force if necessary', section 102(1) of the CA 1989. Other conditions cannot specifically be enforced, but their breach can be justification for bringing the matter back before the court for an application to discharge the supervision order, to seek a care order or for a different order to be made.

The Court of Appeal has held that if a local authority wants to substitute care for supervision, it needs a specific application for a care order and the threshold criteria in section 31 of the CA 1989 must be proved in support of the care application, *Re A (Minor) (Supervision Extension)* [1995] 2 FCR 114, CA.

7.10 Removal of child from care

Local authorities have a duty to look after and maintain children subject to care orders while they are in force, section 33(1) of the CA 1989. A parent, or anyone else, may not remove a child from the care of the local authority without leave of the court. Removal of a child without permission of the local authority or leave of the court, keeping a child away from local authority care or inciting a child to run away or stay away are classed as the criminal offence of child abduction under section 49.

Note that if children are accommodated on a voluntary basis by a local authority (under section 20 of the CA 1989), the situation is different in that they may be removed at any time by a person with parental responsibility for them. A local authority has no power to keep a child in voluntary accommodation where there is a person with parental responsibility ready and willing to look after the child, section 20(7)(8).

7.11 Variation, discharge and appeals

Care orders cease when the child reaches the age of 18, or earlier by order of the court, section 91(2) of the CA 1989.

Supervision orders cease when directed by the court or on effluxion of time.

7.11.1 Variation and discharge

Applicant

A care or supervision order may be varied or discharged on the application of:

(a)   any person with parental responsibility for the child;

(b)   the child (who does not need leave of the court);

(c)   in the case of supervision, the supervisor;

(d)   in the case of a care order, the local authority with the responsibility for the child.

The application needs to be on form C1. Leave, if required, is on form C2, with a draft application in form C1 attached. The court should be that which made the original order. Other courts may accept the application if made with good reason.

Like other applications relating to care orders, once made, the application may only be withdrawn with leave of the court, see rule 29.4 of the FPR 2010.

If the court discharges a care order it can order supervision, without having to re-prove the criteria in section 31(2) of the CA 1989, section 39(4) and (5).

Following an unsuccessful application to discharge a care order, there is no further application without leave within six months, section 91(5) of the CA 1989. Under section 91(14), which can be used regarding any application under the CA 1989, the court can order no further applications without leave, but should use this power sparingly, *Re A (A Child)* [2009] EWCA Civ 1548. Guidelines on the use of section 91(14) are set out in *Re P (A Child)* [1999] EWCA Civ 1323.

Notice

Applications for discharge should be made on notice. The applicant should serve each person entitled to notice with form C6A, with the date and time of the hearing endorsed on it, at least seven days before first directions or hearing. See PD 12C accompanying the FPR 2010. Those entitled to notice are the same as for the original application.

Respondents

Those who are entitled to be respondents should be served with a notice of the proceedings in form C6, together with a draft of the application on form C1, at least seven days before the first directions or hearing. See rule 4(1)(b) of the Family Proceedings Courts (Children Act 1989) Rules 1991, SI 1991/1395 and rule 4.4(1)(b) of the FPR 1991.

Those entitled to be respondents are those who were entitled to be, or were, respondents in the original application.

7.11.2 Appeals

Appeals against decisions concerning care orders lie from the FPC and the county court district judge to the circuit judge, and from the county court circuit judge to the Court of Appeal, see Chapter 17.

On refusal to make a care order, or on discharge, the court has power to make a care order pending appeal, section 40(1) and (2) of the CA 1989; or to declare that the order appealed shall not take effect pending appeal, section 40(3). If the court of first instance refuses to make a care order pending appeal, the appeal court may make an interim care under section 38.

Details of the procedure for permission to appeal to the Supreme Court are set out in the Supreme Court Rules 2009, SI 2009/1603 and there are also explanations on the Supreme Court's website.

7.12 Effects of the Human Rights Act 1998 on care and supervision proceedings

Public authorities must comply with the Human Rights Act 1998 and the ECHR. Any acts by public authorities incompatible with these may be challenged by complaint, appeal or judicial review.

Failure to act is a ground for complaint or challenge, see sections 6 and 7 of the Human Rights Act 1998. Section 22(4) allows retrospective challenge of acts which occurred before the Human Rights Act 1989 came into force.

Article 6 (right to a fair trial) of the ECHR may provide an opportunity to encourage the involvement of children and families in decision making within care planning.

Article 8 of the ECHR gives the right to respect for family life, home and correspondence. It is therefore relevant to the interpretation of current law on contact, family involvement in care plans and care of children, post-adoption contact and the rights of children and their parents in the context of residential care.

The European Court of Human Rights has made it clear that the state authority must make all efforts to reunite a child with his or her family. Under Article 8(2) of the ECHR the right to family life can be interfered with to the extent of permanent separation only when the child's welfare demands this, *KA v Finland* [2003] 1 FCR 230 and *R v Finland* [2006] 2 FCR 264.

Since April 2009 the family courts became more open to the media (with judicial control), and the long-term influence of this on child and family litigation has yet to be seen. Rule 27.11(2) of the FPR 2010 provides 'duly accredited representatives of news gathering and reporting organisations' with a right to attend private hearings in family proceedings, although they can be excluded on specified grounds. However, journalists (and others) are not permitted to publish information they hear during the proceedings without permission of the court (section 12 of the Administration of Justice Act 1960) nor to identify a child in CA 1989 proceedings (section 97 of the CA 1989).

8 Secure Accommodation

Local authorities have a duty to provide accommodation for children in need in circumstances specified in section 20 of the Children Act 1989 (CA 1989) and may otherwise provide accommodation to safeguard or promote the welfare of a child. Secure accommodation is defined in section 25(1) as 'accommodation provided for the purpose of restricting liberty'.

Currently, the law relating to secure accommodation is complex, and in need of clarification. Children aged between 13 and 18 can be placed in secure accommodation for a variety of reasons. They may have committed a criminal offence and need to have their liberty restricted for their own safety or that of others. Orders made in these circumstances are called 'secure orders', to distinguish them from the orders made in civil cases. Children being detained for certain grave crimes are not eligible for secure orders, see para 8.1.2.

A child who is looked after by a local authority, or subject to a care order, may be kept in secure accommodation by the power given by a court order under section 25 of the CA 1989. In certain circumstances, a child may be kept in secure accommodation by the consent of parents or those with parental responsibility.

Secure accommodation is currently governed by section 25 of the CA 1989, the Children (Secure Accommodation) Regulations 1991, SI 1991/1505 (Secure Accommodation Regulations), the Children (Secure Accommodation) (No 2) Regulations 1991, SI 1991/2034 and *The Children Act 1989 Guidance and Regulations* (DCSF) (*Guidance and Regulations*), Volume 5 *Children's Homes*, Chapter 4, and Volume 1 *Court Orders*.

Secure accommodation should be based on the needs of the child, never because of inadequacies of staffing or resources in residential accommodation, nor because a child is being a nuisance. It may never be used as a punishment, see *Guidance and Regulations*, Volume 1 *Court Orders*, paragraphs 5.1–5.3.

Also, *Guidance and Regulations*, Volume 5 *Children's Homes*, paragraph 2.107, provides that restricting the liberty of children is a serious step and a child's liberty can only be restricted in a children's home approved by the Secretary of State as a secure children's home. It is unacceptable for a home that is not approved by the Secretary of State to lock a child in for the purposes of detention.

A child below the age of 13 may not be kept in secure accommodation without the authority of the Secretary of State, regulation 13(4) of the Secure Accommodation Regulations. Children over 16 years of age may not be kept in secure accommodation and wards of court may only be placed in secure accommodation with a direction from the wardship judge.

Secure accommodation is not incompatible with the European Convention for the Protection of Human Rights and Fundamental Freedoms 1950 (ECHR). The ECHR allows minors to be detained by lawful order for the purpose of educational provision. The courts must ensure that any secure accommodation order makes educational provision. Failure to do so would be in breach of the ECHR, see *Re K (Secure Accommodation Order: Right to Liberty)* [2001] 1 FLR 526.

There are useful practice guidelines from the Secure Accommodation Network available at www.secureaccommodation.org.uk.

8.1   Restricting liberty with a secure accommodation order

The effect of a secure accommodation order is to restrict a child's liberty. Local authorities should pay careful regard to the guidance in their use of restriction of liberty. There is a distinction between placing a child in an environment (secure unit), from which he cannot run away and in which he is safeguarded, and the temporary restriction of a child's liberty, for example, locking him in a room, something which is not allowed in mainstream residential care units. It is, however, permissible in certain circumstances to use approved forms of physical restraint as part of a structured behavioural management strategy in order to protect a child or young person from hurting themselves or others, but not to prevent a child from leaving a room or (if the child is of sufficient age) a building unless there is an immediate risk of serious harm.

Guidance and Regulations, Volume 5 *Children's Homes*, paragraph 2.109, provides that 'semi-secure' children's homes have no basis in law. It states that an establishment is either using its premises for the purpose of providing care in a setting which restricts the liberty of a child and has been approved by the Secretary of State as a secure children's home or it is not. Placing authorities, parents or even young people themselves cannot give their own consents for a child to have his or her liberty restricted. Therapy and behaviour management do not provide a reasonable excuse for restricting the liberty of a child in a children's home which is not approved as secure accommodation.

8.1.1 Safeguards

The making of secure accommodation orders is subject to stricter regulation. Some of the key safeguards are as follows:

(a) *Guidance and Regulations*, Volume 5 *Children's Homes*, paragraph 4.7, provides that 'restricting the liberty of a child is a serious step which should only be taken where it is necessary and where other alternatives have been considered'. It goes on to state that 'this does not mean that all other alternatives must have been tried, but instead where a child's liberty is restricted under section 25 of the CA 1989, it is vital that the decision is made on the basis that it is the best option to meet the particular needs of the child'.

(b) *Guidance and Regulations*, Volume 5 *Children's Homes*, paragraph 4.8, provides that secure placements, once made, should only continue for as long as they remain appropriate to meet the needs of the child. Clear plans need to be in place for when the child leaves secure accommodation, to ensure continuity of care and of education and, where necessary, of any specialist intervention or support when the child leaves the home.

(c) Regular inspection and review by:

    (i) Secretary of State (to approve secure unit);

    (ii) Social Services Inspectorate (general running and facilities);

    (iii) Department for Education (educational facilities);

    (iv) Regional Placements Committee (placements);

    (v) Secure Accommodation Review Committee (resources).

(d) Time limits on the duration of secure accommodation orders.

(e) Care plans required by court on review of the orders.

(f) Each child has the right to an independent visitor.

(g) The 'three wise men (or women)'.

The local authority keeping a child in a secure unit must appoint at least three people, one of whom must not be a local authority employee, to review the placement within one month, and thereafter at three-monthly intervals. The task of these three people is to ensure that the criteria justifying secure accommodation still applies, that the placement is necessary and that no other description of accommodation is appropriate. See regulation 15 of the Secure Accommodation Regulations, and *Guidance and Regulations*, Volume 5 *Children's Homes*, paragraphs 4.40–4.46. The local authority must keep good case records, with details listed in regulation 17 and *Guidance and Regulations*, Volume 5 *Children's Homes*, paragraphs 4.47–4.48. The safeguards in section 25 of the CA 1989 also cover children accommodated in independent hospitals and care homes (*Guidance and Regulations*, Volume 5 *Children's Homes*, paragraph 4.33).

With secure orders, the complication in the law is that the routes to the order and the rules applicable vary according to the court to which the child has been remanded. The grounds for the application in each of these circumstances are set out in para 8.3, and procedures in para 8.4.

8.1.2 Criminal cases (secure orders)

Guidance and Regulations, Volume 5 *Children's Homes*, paragraph 4.36 provides that section 25 of the CA 1989 applies with modifications to two groups of children defined in regulation 6(1) of the Secure Accommodation Regulations. These are, firstly, those under section 23 of the Children and Young Persons Act 1969 and, secondly, under section 38 of the Police and Criminal Evidence Act 1984 (PACE). These are considered in turn below.

In criminal proceedings, a child may be remanded or bailed to local authority accommodation under section 23 of the Children and Young Persons Act 1969. Once there, the child may behave in such a way that there is concern that the child may abscond, or injure himself or others. If this concern is justified, then the local authority or other named persons (see para 8.4) may seek a secure order.

Note that children detained pursuant to section 53 of the Children and Young Persons Act 1933 (punishment for certain grave crimes) may not be subject to a secure order.

Juveniles may be detained by the police under circumstances specified in section 38 of PACE and under section 38(6), the juvenile shall be moved to local authority accommodation unless the custody officer certifies that either it is impracticable to do so or, in the case of a juvenile over 12 years old, no secure accommodation is available and other local authority accommodation would not be adequate to protect the public from serious harm from him. Therefore, the remands of juveniles to local authority accommodation by the police in this way are covered by the provisions of section 25 of the CA 1989. There are also safeguards for young people arrested, protecting their interests in detention and during questioning.

Guidance and Regulations, Volume 5 *Children's Homes*, paragraph 4.38, sets out that for both groups of children referred to above, the criteria in section 25(1) of the CA 1989 are therefore applicable.

Under section 130 of the Criminal Justice Act 1988, if juvenile offenders are remanded to local authority accommodation, and placed in secure units, their time so spent will be deducted from their eventual custodial sentence. See also LAC (88)23, which reminds local authorities to keep accurate records of the duration of detention of children in secure units for the sentencing court.

8.1.3   Use of secure accommodation in civil cases

Every local authority is under a duty to 'take reasonable steps designed to avoid the need for children within their area to be placed in secure accommodation'. See Schedule 2, paragraph 7(c) to the CA 1989. Local authorities also have a duty to 'encourage children within their area not to commit criminal offences', see Schedule 2, paragraph 7(b). The local authority looking after the child is under a duty to safeguard and promote the child's welfare, section 22(2). Note, in particular, section 22G requires local authorities to take such steps, as far as are reasonably practicable, to ensure that there is sufficient accommodation in their area which meets the needs of looked after children. See also in this context, *Putting Care into Practice; Statutory Guidance for Local Authorities in Care Planning, Placement and Case Review for Looked after Children* (DfE, 2010) and *Guidance and Regulations*, Volume 2 *Care Planning, Placement and Case Review*.

8.2   How long can a child be kept in secure accommodation?

8.2.1   Where no court order made

Without the authority of the court, a child may only have his liberty restricted for up to 72 hours, either consecutively or in aggregate within any period of 28 consecutive days, regulation 10(1) of the Secure Accommodation Regulations. However, pursuant to *Guidance and Regulations*, Volume 5 *Children's Homes*, paragraph 4.20, this limit to 72 hours is given some limited flexibility by virtue of regulation 10(3), so as to meet the difficulties which may be faced by local authorities in arranging for secure applications to be heard at short notice, in circumstances where the 72 hours period expires late on Saturday, a Sunday or public holiday.

Where a child has been placed in local authority accommodation on a voluntary basis under section 20(1) of the CA 1989, a person with parental responsibility can remove the child at any time, section 20(8), unless the exceptions in section 20(9) apply. This includes removal from secure accommodation.

8.2.2   Secure order (child on remand in a criminal case)

Where the child has been remanded by a criminal court, the duration is for the period of the remand, with a maximum order of 28 days, regulation 13 of the Secure Accommodation Regulations.

Regulation 10(2) of the Secure Accommodation Regulations, however, gives an exception where, if the court authorises secure accommodation for less than 28 days, on the day when the court order expires, the 28-day period mentioned in regulation 10(1) starts running afresh from that day, ignoring any time spent in secure accommodation before the court order. Regulation 10(3) gives special provisions for days either side of public holidays by granting a limited extension of the 72-hour time limit.

8.2.3   Civil cases and children not on criminal remand – secure accommodation orders

If the child is not on remand, or committed to the Crown Court, then the maximum period is:

- up to three months on the first application, regulation 11 of the Secure Accommodation Regulations, and

- up to six months on subsequent applications, regulation 12.

The period of detention runs from the date the order was made, not the date the child was actually placed in the unit, see *Re B (Minor) (Secure Accommodation)* [1994] 2 FLR 707.

Any period in the secure unit before a secure accommodation order is made should be deducted from this, *C (Minor) v Humberside CC and Another* [1995] 1 FCR 110, in which the justices making a care order had no power to order that a child kept in secure accommodation for a month should then be kept in the secure unit for a further three months.

In the case of *In Re W (Minor) (Secure Accommodation Order)* [1993] 1 FLR 692 it was held that the court should consider the shortest appropriate period, rather than order the maximum period available as a matter of course.

Also, in *R v Oxfordshire County Council (Secure Accommodation)* [1992] Fam 150, [1992] 3 All ER 660, it was decided that once an order is made, it should only be for so long as is necessary and unavoidable.

If the criteria for detention in secure accommodation cease to apply, the child must be released, *LM v Essex CC* [1999] 1 FLR 988. Therefore, the local authority could not lawfully continue to keep a child in secure accommodation within the maximum period specified in the order at a time when it did not consider the criteria under section 25 of the CA 1989 continued to be met. The remedy for the child was an application to the High Court for a writ of *habeas corpus*.

8.2.4 Adjournments

If there is an adjournment of an application for secure accommodation, then, under section 25(5) of the CA 1989, the court may permit the child to be kept secure during the adjournment. There is here an obvious risk of getting the order sought by the back door, perhaps without adequate proof of its necessity, particularly if the adjournment is for further evidence to become available.

In the case of *Birmingham City Council v M* [2008] EWHC 1085 (Fam), the court held that the court could not adjourn a secure accommodation application solely in order to keep the children's guardian and solicitor engaged in the case and supporting the child. Furthermore, if the adjournment was not justified (e.g. to obtain further information or for reasons of procedural fairness), then the court should hold the substantive hearing. This followed on from the previous decision in *Re B (A Minor) (Secure Accommodation)* [1994] 2 FLR 707.

8.3 Grounds for application

8.3.1 Children remanded in criminal cases

Where a child has been remanded by a criminal court to local authority accommodation, under section 23 of the Children and Young Persons Act 1969, or the child is detained under section 38(6) of PACE, then the child may be the subject of an application for secure accommodation under section 25 of the CA 1989.

If the young person was remanded by a youth court, then the application under section 25 of the CA 1989 should be made to the youth court, and if remanded by the magistrates' court, application should be made to the magistrates' court.

If the young person was remanded by the Crown Court, then application should be made to the family proceedings court (FPC).

Section 23 of the Children and Young Persons Act 1969 applies to children who are:

(a)   charged with or convicted of an offence which would carry a sentence of 14 years or more for a person aged over 21;

(b)   charged with or convicted of an offence of violence, or who have a previous conviction for violence;

(c)   detained under section 38(6) of PACE 1984.

For the purposes of criminal secure accommodation cases, a child who is remanded to local authority accommodation under section 23 of the Children and Young Persons Act 1969 can be subject to a secure order, but only if the child is charged with, or convicted of, certain offences punishable, in the case of a person aged 21 or over, for 14 years or more, or the child has a recent history of absconding while remanded to local authority accommodation, and is charged with, or has been convicted of, an imprisonable offence alleged or found to have been committed whilst he was on remand, see *Guidance and Regulations*, Volume 5 *Children's Homes*, paragraphs 4.36–4.38.

These children, if remanded to local authority accommodation, are subject to regulation 6(2) of the Secure Accommodation Regulations, which provides that a child may not be kept in secure accommodation unless it appears that any accommodation other than that provided for the purpose of restricting his liberty is inappropriate because:

(a)   the child is likely to abscond from such accommodation;

(b)   the child is likely to injure himself or other people if he is kept in any such accommodation.

Note that the likelihood of significant harm is omitted in this regulation.

If the criteria are satisfied, then the order must be made. The welfare of the child is not the paramount consideration in this situation.

The criteria for children in civil cases is slightly different, see para 8.3.2.

8.3.2   Children in civil cases

Children who are looked after by a local authority accommodated in care homes, independent hospitals, nursing homes, mental nursing homes, or accommodated by health authorities, Primary Care Trusts,

National Health Service Trusts, or local authorities in the exercise of education functions, are subject to the provisions of section 25 of the CA 1989. See regulation 7 of the Secure Accommodation Regulations.

Section 25 of the CA 1989 provides that if:

(a) (i) the child has a history of absconding and is likely to abscond from any other description of accommodation; and

(ii) if he absconds he is likely to suffer significant harm; or

(b) that if he is kept in any other description of accommodation, he is likely to injure himself or others,

the child can be placed in local authority accommodation by the court.

In the case of *Re M (A Minor) (Secure Accommodation Order)* [1995] 2 FCR 373, the welfare of the child was held by the court to be relevant, but not paramount in proceedings under section 25 of the CA 1989, and therefore application of the welfare checklist, although useful, was not obligatory.

A child may be placed in a secure unit under section 25(1) of the CA 1989 to prevent her injuring another child, which may be inconsistent with putting the welfare of the secured child first. The court's duty mirrors that of the local authority under section 20(1)(b). The court must ascertain whether the section 25 conditions are satisfied, and if so, to make the order if this accords with the duty of the local authority to safeguard and promote the welfare of the child. The children's guardian will assist the court in deciding these questions, *Re M (Secure Accommodation Order)* [1995] Fam 108, [1995] 3 All ER 407.

If the child is voluntarily accommodated by the local authority, i.e. not subject to a care order) a person with parental responsibility may remove the child from the secure accommodation at any time, see sections 20(8), (9) and 25(9) of the CA 1989.

8.4 Practice and procedure

Secure accommodation orders are not included in the definition of 'family proceedings' in section 8 of the CA 1989, but because section 92(2) says that 'all proceedings under the Act shall be treated as family proceedings in relation to magistrates' courts', this means that in the FPC, section 25 applications are included. The menu of orders available in family proceedings is therefore open to the court, including section 8 orders and others which the court can make of its own initiative (see Figure 6).

8.4.1   Application

Where a child is being looked after by a local authority (even if the child is accommodated by another body) that local authority should be the applicant for the order. In other circumstances, other potential applicants include those who are providing accommodation for the child, that is:

- local authority;
- health authority or NHS Trust;
- local education authority;
- person running a residential home, independent hospital, nursing home, or a nursing home for the mentally ill.

Once made, an application may only be withdrawn with leave of the court.

8.4.2   Forms

The application should be made on form C1 together with form C20 in accordance with PD 5A accompanying the FPR 2010.

If the application is made to the High Court in wardship, it should be by summons and the ward should be named as a party. It is suggested that it should be made by invoking the court's inherent jurisdiction by using form C66, see PD 5A accompanying the FPR 2010.

8.4.3   Venue

An application for an order under section 25 of the CA 1989 may be made only to the FPC, unless there are existing proceedings in a higher court (paragraph 5 of the Allocation and Transfer of Proceedings Order 2008, SI 2008/28). Secure accommodation orders can be made at any level of the court. They can be made in criminal proceedings at the youth court or at a higher level of criminal court; and in the FPC, the county court or High Court in the course of other proceedings. Pursuant to Article 5(2)(c) of the Allocation and Transfer of Proceedings Order 2008, in the case of a civil secure order, the proceedings should be commenced in the FPC, unless there are pending proceedings in another court, in which case the application should be made in that court.

8.4.4 Respondents

Respondents should be served with a copy of the application in form C1 with form C20, and form C6 notice of the proceedings with the date and place of hearing, rule 12.8 of the FPR 2010 and the accompanying PD 12C, paragraph 1.1(1).

Service should be one day before the hearing, PD 12C, paragraph 2.1(6) accompanying the FPR 2010.

Pursuant to rule 12.3 of the FPR 2010, certain people are automatically respondents to the application:

(a) those believed to have parental responsibility for the child;

(b) those who had parental responsibility prior to the care order, if one is in force;

(c) the child.

Others may be joined as respondents, and automatic respondents may be removed by direction of the court. See rules 12.3(3) and 16.2 of the FPR 2010.

8.4.5 Notice

Applications for secure accommodation must be made on one day's notice, PD 12C, paragraph 2.1(6) accompanying the FPR 2010.

The following people are entitled to notice of the proceedings, with the date, time and place of the hearing:

(a) a local authority providing accommodation for the child;

(b) any person with whom the child was living at the time proceedings were commenced;

(c) person providing a refuge for the child under section 51 of the CA 1989, see rule 12.8 of the FPR 2010 and the accompanying PD 12C.

Regulation 14 of the Secure Accommodation Regulations provides a list of people who should be informed of the application as soon as practicable if the child is placed in a secure unit in a community home, and the application is to keep the child there:

(a) the child's parents;

(b) any person with parental responsibility for the child;

(c)   the child's independent visitor;

(d)   any other person the local authority considers should be told.

8.4.6 Service

Service is effected on a solicitor for a party by delivery at his office, by first class post at the office or through the DX, by fax to the office or through any other means of electronic communication in accordance with PD 6A accompanying the FPR 2010, see rule 6.23 of the FPR 2010.

Service on a party who has no solicitor is by delivery to that party personally, or by delivery of first class post to his address, see rules 6.28–6.33 of the FPR 2010.

Service on a child may be through her solicitor or the children's guardian, or, with leave of the court, service on the child herself, see rules 6.28–6.33 of the FPR 2010.

The time for service may be abridged by the court, or waived altogether, see rule 4.1(3)(a) of the FPR 2010.

8.5 Role of the children's guardian

These proceedings are 'specified proceedings' within the meaning of section 41 of the CA 1989 and therefore a children's guardian must be appointed by the court unless it is of the opinion that it is unnecessary to do so in order to safeguard the child's interests. This is a protective measure intended to ensure that children in secure units have had their wishes and feelings made known to the court, and that the court has been advised of the most appropriate way forward in the best interests of the child. Children who are accommodated on a voluntary basis under section 20(1) are also safeguarded by this provision.

8.6 Contact

Children in secure units have the right to reasonable contact with members of their family, as children in care (see Chapter 7, para 7.6.4 and Chapter 12, para 12.5). Since an application under section 25 of the CA 1989 in a magistrates' court amounts to 'family proceedings' under section 8, provided there is no care order in force, it is possible for the court to make a section 8 contact order to run alongside the secure accommodation order. A section 8 contact order can also co-exist with a supervision order. If the child is in care, then a section 34 care contact order may be made if necessary.

8.7   Rights of the child

The rights of the child are as follows:

- three persons to review placement, regulation 15 of the Secure Accommodation Regulations;
- duty on local authority to keep detailed case records, regulation 17;
- education whilst accommodated;
- entitlement to appropriate therapy where necessary;
- regular inspection of the secure unit by the Social Services Inspectorate from the Department of Health, who must approve the unit;
- inspection by the Department for Education, because children there are receiving education whilst accommodated;
- regional placement committees, who check the resources and conditions of the unit;
- time limits on the duration of secure accommodation orders;
- care plans on review of the orders;
- independent visitor;
- consultation, and to have wishes and feelings ascertained, section 22(4) of the CA 1989;
- consultation with parents and those with parental responsibility, section 22(4); and
- 'free' public finding to be represented on section 25 application.

In relation to the detailed case records referred to above, *Guidance and Regulations*, Volume 5 *Children's Homes*, paragraph 4.47 makes specific reference to regulation 17 of the Secure Accommodation Regulations, which sets out details as to the contents. They must include, amongst other matters, details as to the statutory provision under which the child is in secure accommodation, date, time of the placement, reason for the placement, name of officer authorising the placement and details of the reviews undertaken.

In relation to secure criteria reviews, regulation 15 of the Secure Accommodation Regulations 1991 provides that the first review must be held within one month of the start of the placement, and thereafter reviews must take place at intervals not exceeding three months.

Regulation 16(1) of the Secure Accommodation Regulations requires the persons appointed to be satisfied as to whether or not the criteria for keeping the child in secure accommodation continue to apply and as to whether any other type of accommodation would be appropriate for the child. The child's wishes and feelings, as far as is practicable, need to be taken into account, as well as in particular that of the child's parent, any other person who has parental responsibility for the child, and of anyone else who has had the care of the child. The views of the child's independent visitor, where one has been appointed, also need to be considered, as well as that of the local authority managing the secure accommodation in which the child is placed, if not managed by the local authority looking after the child.

Children and young people subject to applications have the right to be present in court. Rule 12.14(3) of the FPR 2010 gives the court power to exclude a child who wants to attend court if it is in the child's interest to do so and he or she is represented, although rule 12.14(4) requires the court to give the guardian, the child's solicitor and child, if of sufficient understanding, the opportunity to make representations about the child's attendance. In *Re K (A Child)* [2011] EWHC 1082, the court held that there is no presumption that a child should not attend. The only reason to prevent the attendance of a child who wishes to attend is if attendance may cause her psychological damage.

8.7.1   Public funding

Public funding is available to a child subject to application under section 25 of the CA 1989, who wishes to be legally represented. Public funding therefore for secure accommodation cases is 'free', that is, non-means and non-merits tested.

In *The Funding Code* (Legal Services Commission, 2011), Chapter 20, paragraph 2 entitled 'Children and Family: Public Law Proceedings' provides that funding for an application for a Secure Accommodation order comes within the same category as those applications that come within the definition of 'Special Children Act proceedings'. These are defined in section 2.2 of *The Funding Code Criteria* as including essentially proceedings under section 31 of the CA 1989 (i.e. for care and supervision orders), section 43 (child assessment orders), section 44 (emergency protection orders) and section 45 (extension or discharge of an emergency protection order). For these, representation of children, parents and those with parental responsibility is available without reference to means, prospects of success or reasonableness. *The Funding*

Code does provide that full representation will not be necessary for the child if he or she is already represented in criminal proceedings to which the section 25 application relates, as the criminal legal aid order will cover proceedings under section 25 as well.

Also note that applications for public funding for parents in secure accommodation cases may be refused on the basis that their legal representation is not necessary as representations will be made by both the local authority and the advocate on behalf of the child.

8.7.2 Right to legal advice

Section 25(6) of the CA 1989 provides that the court hearing the application cannot make the secure order unless the child is legally represented, except where he has been informed of his right to legal advice, and had the opportunity, but failed or refused to apply. If a child is not notified of the application for the secure order, the matter may not be heard, as set out in *Re AS* [1999] 1 FLR 103, in which the court decided that natural justice required notification to the child of the application. However, in the later case of *Re C (Secure Accommodation Order: Representation)* [2001] 1 FLR 857, the Family Division decided that the decision to hear the secure application was not outside a reasonable exercise of the court's discretion.

8.7.3 Age of child

There are particular rules surrounding secure application for younger children. Most notably, if the child is under 13 years of age, then the permission of the Secretary of State is required before a secure order can be made, regulation 4 of the Secure Accommodation Regulations.

Also, if the child is over 16 years of age, and is also accommodated under section 20(5) of the CA 1989, then an application for secure accommodation cannot be commenced in respect of the child. However, if an application had been commenced prior to the child's 16th birthday, then a secure order can be made, which can then continue beyond the birthday for that child, *Re G (Secure Accommodation)* [2000] 2 FLR 259.

8.8 Appeals and the Human Rights Act 1998

Appeals in family proceedings are governed by Part 30 of the FPR 2010, as well as the accompanying PD 30A, which provides a codified procedure for appeals. It does not cover appeals to the Court of

Appeal or the Supreme Court, both of which are covered by Part 52 of the Civil Procedure Rules 1998, SI 1998/3132.

Section 94 of the CA 1989 makes provision for appeals from the FPC to a county court as well as appeals to the High Court against decisions or refusals to authorise applications for the restriction of liberty. The placement in secure accommodation may continue whilst an appeal against authorisation is waiting to be determined. If the appeal is against a refusal to authorise, the child may not be detained in a secure unit pending appeal. Appeals from the county court or High Court lie to the Court of Appeal.

An appeal in family cases may normally only be made with the permission of the lower court, or of the appeal court in accordance with rule 30.3(3) and (4) of the FPR 2010. Permission to appeal, therefore, would be required from the decision of a district judge (county court/High Court). However, permission to appeal is not required where the appeal is against a secure accommodation order, rule 30.3(1)(2).

The Human Rights Act 1998 and Article 5 of the ECHR are relevant to decisions of local authorities and the courts in secure accommodation issues. Article 5 confirms the right to liberty and security of a person and Article 8 protects the right to family life. Article 5 refers to the detention of minors for 'educational supervision' or for the purpose of 'bringing them before the competent legal authority'.

Acts of public authorities and the courts which do not comply with the Human Rights Act 1998 or the ECHR may be challenged by complaint, judicial review, or appeal.

9 Education Supervision Orders

Education between 5 and 16 years is compulsory. The Education Act 1996 combined with the provisions of section 36 of and Schedule 3 to the CA 1989, authorises prosecution of parents who fail to ensure that their child receives a proper full-time education. A local authority has an obligation under section 444 (A and ZA) of the Education Act 1996 to take legal action so as to enforce school attendance. This will be done through its Education Welfare Service.

Parents have the right to educate their children other than in school, provided that the child receives a 'proper education' as described below. The local education authority may agree, under the Education Act 1996, to help parents to arrange education otherwise than at school.

Section 36(4) of the CA 1989 states that 'a child is being properly educated only if he is receiving efficient full-time education suitable to his age, ability and aptitude, and any special educational needs he may have'. Under section 437 of the Education Act 1996, a local education authority which is concerned about a child's education may serve notice on parents to show that the child is being properly educated. If the parents fail to comply or to provide the required proof, then the local education authority may serve on parents a 'school attendance order', requiring the parents to register the child at a named school. Failure to comply with this order constitutes an offence, and on prosecution, the court may direct the local education authority to apply for an education supervision order.

9.1 Effects of an education supervision order

An education supervision order, made under section 36 of the CA 1989 places the child under the supervision of a local education authority. These differ from supervision orders made under section 31. School refusal is no longer by itself a ground for care, but it may be evidence of neglect, lack of parental control, underlying emotional problems, or that the education system may be failing to meet the needs of the child. School refusal may, therefore, form part of the section 31 grounds, see Chapter 7, and *Re O (A Minor) (Care Order: Education Procedure)* [1992] 2 FLR 7.

Schedule 3, paragraph 12(1) to the CA 1989 sets out the supervisor's duty to 'advise, assist and befriend and give directions to the supervised child and to his parents', 'in such as way as will ... secure that he is properly educated'.

Schedule 3, paragraph 12(3) to the CA 1989 provides that the supervisor should take into account the wishes and feelings of the child and parents, directions made should be reasonable and such that the parents and child are able to comply with them. Persistent failure to comply with directions may lead to prosecution.

Schedule 3, paragraph 18(2) to the CA 1989 sets out the defences to a prosecution for failure to comply with a school attendance order, which includes: showing that all reasonable steps were taken to comply; that the directions were unreasonable; that there was compliance with directions or requirements in a supervision order; and that it was not reasonably practicable to comply with both the supervision order and the school attendance order.

Directions might require the child to attend meetings with the supervisor or with teachers at the school to discuss progress, or cover medical assessment or examination, or assessment by a clinical psychologist. They should be confirmed in writing, and the parents informed.

Under Schedule 3, paragraph 13 to the CA 1989, parents lose their right to have the child educated at home or to move the child to another school while an education supervision order is in force, and they have no right of appeal against admissions decisions.

9.2 Duration

The order will subsist for one year, or until the child is no longer of compulsory school age, whichever is the earlier, Schedule 3, paragraph 15(1) and (6) to the CA 1989. It may be discharged earlier, on the application of the child, the parents, or the local education authority, Schedule 3, paragraph 17(1).

It may be extended for up to three years if application is made within three months before the expiry date, and it can be extended more than once, Schedule 3, paragraph 15 to the CA 1989. It will cease on the making of a care order, Schedule 3, paragraph 15(6)(b).

9.3   Grounds for application

Under section 36(3) of the CA 1989, an order may only be made if the court is 'satisfied that the child concerned is of compulsory school age and is not being properly educated'; section 36(4) states that 'a child is being properly educated only if he is receiving efficient full time education suitable to his age, ability and aptitude, and any special educational needs he may have'.

Where a child is the subject to a school attendance order under section 437 of the Education Act 1996 which is in force but with which the child is not complying, or is a registered pupil of a school which he is not attending regularly within the meaning of section 444; there is a presumption that the child is not being properly educated, see section 36(5) of the CA 1989.

Note that an order may not be sought in respect of a child who is already subject to a care order, section 36(6) of the CA 1989.

Before making an application for an education supervision order, the local education authority is required under section 36(8) of the CA 1989 to consult social services.

A recent publication entitled *Improving attendance at school* (DfE, 2012) by Charlie Taylor, the government's Expert Adviser on Behaviour, provides an important insight into the difficulties surrounding school attendance. *Improving attendance at school*, paragraph 19 refers to parental sanctions and states that '… Fining parents or taking them to court is a last resort that schools and EWOs use only very reluctantly when all else has failed. However, when they do so the system must be efficient and effective'.

Improving attendance at school, paragraph 20 states that:

> When attendance falls schools can use the legal system to punish parents who fail in this duty, but this process is protracted and inconsistent. For most schools and LAs legal intervention is the end of a process that has seen the parent and child offered a range of support. Schools or local authorities may impose a fixed penalty notice (FPN) on parents whose child is not attending regularly. The parent has 28 days to pay a fine of £50; if they fail then it is doubled. After 42 days if the parent has not paid then the school or LA has to withdraw the penalty notice and the parent is then prosecuted under section 444 of the Education Act 1996. Currently 50–60 per cent of FPNs are paid.

One of the closing remarks in *Improving attendance at school*, paragraph 33 is, 'One of the most effective ways that schools can improve achievement is by improving attendance. Even the very best teachers struggle to raise the standards of children who are not in school regularly. Schools that relentlessly pursue good attendance also get better overall attainment and behaviour'.

The children's services department may seek the assistance of the education authority in the provision of services for the child, which is under a duty to comply with the request in accordance with section 27(1)–(3) of the CA 1989.

9.4 Practice and procedure

9.4.1 Application

The applicant is the local education authority under section 36(6) of the CA 1989. The application should be made on form C17 with supplement C179, see PD 5A accompanying the FPR 2010. Applications to renew an order are made on forms C17A and C110.

Applications are 'family proceedings' under section 8(3) and (4) of the CA 1989, and therefore the menu of orders is available to the court (see Figure 6). The principles in section 1 apply, see Chapter 2. An application may not be made in respect of a child subject to a care order, section 36(6).

9.4.2 Venue

Cases should be commenced in the family proceedings court (FPC), but may be transferred to the county court or the High Court, pursuant to Articles 14–19 of the Allocation and Transfer of Proceedings Order 2008, SI 2008/28. If the county court or the High Court has directed an investigation of the child's circumstances under section 37(1) of the CA 1989, the application may be made to that court. If there are proceedings pending in a court, then the application may commence there.

9.4.3 Notice

PD 12A accompanying the FPR 2010, provides that seven days' notice of the hearing or directions appointment must be given, with the date and venue of the application.

A local authority providing accommodation for the child, or the person with whom a child is living, or the manager of a refuge providing accommodation for the child under section 51 of the CA 1989 may be served with notice of the application, on form C6A, pursuant to PD 12C, paragraph 3.1 accompanying the FPR 2010.

9.4.4 Respondents

Every person with parental responsibility for the child is a respondent, as is the child. Respondents should be served with notice of the application, together with a copy of the application in forms C17 and C1. Both forms are contained in PD 5A accompanying the FPR 2010. Respondents may file and serve an answer two days before the hearing.

9.4.5 Service

The normal rules of service apply, see PD 6A accompanying the FPR 2010 and rule 6.23. The time for service may be abridged by the court, or waived altogether, see rule 4.1(3)(a).

The applicant needs to serve form C9 at or before the hearing, so as to confirm service, when, by whom, and which document(s).

9.5 Rights of the child

The rights of the child are:

(a) the child's welfare is paramount;

(b) to be consulted on schooling issues;

(c) to have wishes and feelings taken into consideration;

(d) to be a respondent in the application if of sufficient age and understanding;

(e) to receive directions that are reasonable;

(f) to advice, assistance and befriending from the supervisor.

9.6 Variation, discharge and appeals

Discharge can be on the application of the child, the parents or the local education authority, Schedule 3, paragraph 17(1) to the CA 1989. The court on discharge may order the local authority to investigate the child's circumstances under section 37 and Schedule 3, paragraph 17(2).

The order may be extended for up to three years on application by the authority within three months before the expiry date, and the order can be extended more than once, Schedule 3, paragraph 15 to the CA 1989.

9.6.1 Appeals

Appeal lies from the FPC to the High Court and from the county court or High Court to the Court of Appeal, see PD 30A accompanying the FPR 2010, which provides a codified procedure for appeals. An appeal may normally only be made with the permission of the lower court, or of the appeal court. Permission to appeal therefore would be required from the decision of a district judge (county court/High Court).

Interestingly, the European Convention for the Protection of Human Rights and Fundamental Freedoms 1950 (ECHR) envisages the use of secure accommodation to detain a minor for 'educational supervision', Article 5 of the ECHR.

However, read in conjunction with Article 8 (right to family life) of the ECHR, it is unlikely that in the UK this would encourage courts to take a step in that direction.

10 Police Powers under the Children Act 1989

The police have special powers under section 46 of the Children Act 1989 (CA 1989) referred to as 'police protection', which do not need a court order. The ground for action is that police have reasonable cause to believe the child would otherwise suffer significant harm, section 46(1).

The Children Act 1989 Guidance and Regulations (DCSF) (*Guidance and Regulations*), Volume 1 *Court Orders*, paragraph 4.69 provides that neither the constable concerned, nor the designated officer acquires parental responsibility for a child who is in police protection following the exercise of powers under section 46 of the CA 1989. The designated officer must nevertheless do what is reasonable in all the circumstances to promote the child's welfare, bearing in mind that the child cannot be kept in police protection for more than 72 hours, section 46(6) and (9).

10.1 Police powers and responsibilities

The special powers of the police are:

- to remove a child to a safe place and keep him there, section 46(1)(a) of the CA 1989;

- to prevent a child's removal from a safe place, section 46(1)(b);

- no power to enter premises without a warrant unless section 17 of the Police and Criminal Evidence Act 1984 satisfied (section 17 includes saving life and limb, prevention of serious damage to property, or arrests);

- to safeguard and promote the child's welfare, section 46(9)(b).

The maximum duration for the exercise of powers under section 46 of the CA 1989 is 72 hours, section 46(6).

Each area must have a 'designated police officer' responsible for carrying out the duties imposed by the CA 1989, who can apply for emergency protection if necessary, section 46(3)(e) and (7).

The police must, under section 46(3) of the CA 1989, inform the local authority of their action, the reasons for it, and the child's whereabouts; inform the child and discover his wishes and feelings; remove the child to local authority accommodation and, under section 46(4), take reasonable steps to inform parents, those with parental responsibility, and those with whom the child was living, of the action, the reasons for it and future plans.

Guidance and Regulations, Volume 1 *Court Orders*, paragraph 4.64 provides that police powers should only be used in exceptional circumstances where there is insufficient time to seek an emergency protection order, or for reasons relating to the immediate safety of the child.

10.2   Contact with child

Pursuant to section 46(10) of the CA 1989, in relation to contact, the designated officer must also allow the following persons to have such contact with the child as, in the officer's opinion, is both reasonable and in the child's best interests:

- the child's parents;

- anyone else who has parental responsibility for the child;

- anyone with whom the child was living immediately before he was taken into police protection;

- anyone who has in his favour an order relating to contact with the child;

- anyone acting on behalf of any of the above.

Note that the case of *A v (1) East Sussex County Council, (2) Chief Constable of Sussex* [2010] EWCA Civ 743 decided that, in appropriate circumstances, an application should be made for an emergency protection order, as opposed to the police exercising powers of police protection.

11 Instructions and Case Preparation in Family Proceedings

Family proceedings are non-adversarial. Advocates may be instructed to represent children, parents, other parties or local authorities. Effective advocacy depends more on thorough preparation of the case, coupled with good negotiation skills with all parties throughout the proceedings, than on the final presentation in court.

The first task is to elicit from all sources available as much information as possible about the circumstances of the case, the client and the child. All evidence relevant to the welfare of the child should be available to the court.

11.1 Action plan on receipt of instructions from an adult or local authority

- Arrange to interview the client or instructing social worker as soon as possible.

- Where appropriate, check the public funding situation and complete the necessary forms.

- Obtain copies of all applications and documents which have been filed with the court.

- Find out whether there other relevant proceedings current or pending. If there are, obtain details.

- Find out whether there have been previous proceedings in relation to the child(ren) or the family. If so, ask for copies of all previous/existing court orders and copies of documents filed with the court. Consent and appropriate directions by the court may be necessary to authorise and facilitate disclosure of documents from another court or from other proceedings.

- Ascertain who the other parties are. Check whether they have instructed legal representatives, and obtain details.

- Identify any other people who should be made parties to the proceedings or notified of the proceedings in accordance with the Rules, and take appropriate action.

- Let the court and all other parties (or their advocates if they are represented) and the children's guardian know you are instructed in the matter, and write, inviting communication and offering co-operation. (See Chapter 15 if you are instructed by the children's guardian on behalf of the child.)

- Interview potential witnesses.

- Follow the *Public Law Outline* (PLO) procedures, or other relevant Practice Directions accompanying the Family Procedure Rules 2010, SI 2010/2955 (FPR 2010).

11.2   Interviewing clients

Cases involving family breakup or issues of child protection are stressful for all the parties concerned. It is essential to establish a relationship of trust with clients, giving them space in the initial interview to express their feelings, whilst at the same time keeping the interview focused on taking background history and instructions. Set aside sufficient time to allow clients to fully express all they have to say and offer appropriate refreshments – this can provide a welcome break. A checklist may assist to keep the interview focused on the information required. Below are sample checklists of some basic issues to cover when interviewing parents, social workers and medical witnesses, to which can be added specific issues relevant to each case.

11.2.1   Checklist for information from parents

- Full name and address.

- Home telephone number. (Any restrictions on its use?)

- Work telephone number. (Any restrictions on its use?)

- Mobile telephone number. (Any restrictions on its use?)

- Names of all the children of the family and their dates of birth.

- Who are the parents of each child of the family?

- Who has parental responsibility for the child?

- Where does each child of the family live, if they do not live with the client?

- What are the present contact arrangements with the children living elsewhere?

- Partner and family members living in client's household. This will be of particular relevance so as to ensure there are appropriate assessments undertaken of 'connected persons', see in particular the assessment process as set out in regulations 24–25 of the Care Planning, Placement and Case Review (England) Regulations 2010, SI 2010/959.

- The family's social/cultural/racial/ religious context.

- Does this client, any member of the family or the child(ren) have any special needs, cultural issues, language difficulties, etc. of which the court, children's guardian and other parties need to be aware? In particular, if there are issues surrounding the client parent having a learning disability, there should be a referral to the adult disability team.

  Also consider whether there may be an issue as to the parent client lacking litigation capacity. If so, there may need for a referral to be made to a psychologist or psychiatrist, so as to assess litigation capacity. This may lead to a possible invitation for the Official Solicitor to become involved, see in particular Part 15 of the FPR 2010, relating to protected parties.

- Obtain general information about this client, including: background, education, attainments, current or past employment, interests and significant life events.

- Does this client or any partner, family member, carer or cohabitee have any convictions for offences which may affect an assessment of their capacity to care for the child(ren)? For example, conviction for an offence listed in Schedule 1 to the Children and Young Persons Act 1933, drink or drugs related offences, etc?

  Note: *Working Together to Safeguard Children, A guide to inter-agency working to safeguard and promote the welfare of children* (DCSF, 2010), paragraphs 12.4–12.5, states that the term 'Schedule One offence' is one that triggers any statutory requirement in relation to child protection issues – the term concentrates solely by the age of the victim and offence for which the offender was sentenced, and not by an assessment of whether the offender may pose a future risk of harm to children. Therefore, the term 'Schedule One offender' is no longer used, and it has been replaced with 'Risk to children'. This term refers to the fact that the person presents a risk, or potential risk, of harm to children.

- Convictions should be disclosed to the court, *Re R (Minors) (Custody)* [1986] 1 FLR 6.

- Does the client or any family member have any particular skills or attributes relevant to their parenting ability?

- Have there been any previous court orders or applications made to a court in respect of this child, or any other child of the family or any family member?

- Other people or bodies involved with the family who may be able to assist in providing information:

    - schools attended by the child(ren)

    - playgroups

    - voluntary organisations/religious organisations

    - therapists

    - GP/hospital

    - health visitor

    - community, religious or other agencies or organisations involved with the family

- How does the client see the present situation? Obtain:

    - details of the circumstances that led up to this application

    - a description of the current situation and presenting problems

    - details of the client's wishes, feelings and concerns

    - the client's instructions as to what he or she wishes to happen in this case (subject to the legal advice the client may receive now or later).

- Does the client have any comments to make or explanations to offer about causation of any injuries or harm alleged, or the child's emotional problems?

- What contact has the client had to date with social services, or other professionals about this child?

- Has the client requested or received any help, advice, or resources from social services?

- What would the client like to see happen in the future concerning the child(ren)?

- What would the child(ren) like to happen?

- What does the client think that others will say about the situation? (Often a very revealing question.)

- Can the client think of others who may be able to offer relevant information about the child or family?

Public Law Outline *requirements on information from local authorities and social workers*

The PLO checklist (as set out in PD 12A accompanying the FPR 2010) is now the one that is used to ensure that social workers and local authorities have provided all the information and documentation that is required of them. There are pro formas and checklists to be followed. Annex A to the PLO has the list of documents to be filed with any application for care or supervision. Annex B sets out the Local Authority's Case Summary. Annex C provides a pro forma for a draft case management order.

The Annex documents to the application form (form C110), where available are:

- social work chronology;

- initial social work statement;

- initial and core assessments;

- letters before proceedings;

- schedule of proposed findings;

- care plan.

The chronology prepared for court and social work statements are factual accounts of recent events leading to the application.

The letter before proceedings sets out in clear terms what is considered to be the problem, see below.

PD 12A accompanying the FPR 2010 also makes reference to other checklist documents which already exist on local authority files, which are to be disclosed in the event of proceedings, normally before the day of the first appointment. These are:

- previous court orders and judgments/reasons;

- any relevant assessment materials;

- section 7 and section 37 reports;

- relatives' and friends' materials (e.g. a genogram);

- other relevant reports and records;

- single, joint or inter-agency materials (e.g. health and education/Home Office and immigration documents);

- records of discussions with the family;

- key local authority minutes and records for the child (including strategy discussion record);

- pre-existing care plans (e.g. child in need plan, looked after child plan and child protection plan).

The Children Act 1989 Guidance and Regulations (DCSF), Volume 1 *Court Orders*, paragraph 3.3 provides that before an application is made for a care or supervision order, the local authority should, in appropriate cases, send a letter before proceedings to the parents, the contents of which should be explained carefully and directly to the parents, taking into account the way in which information is presented in the light of the parents' cognitive and linguistic abilities. The purpose of this letter is to enable the parents to obtain legal assistance and advice, so as to address the concerns. A standard template letter is set out in Volume 1.

Most of the information that the court will require will be contained in the Core Assessment. However, the PLO provides for the filing of records of discussions with the family and key local authority minutes and records for the child, including strategy discussions. See Chapter 7 and P Pressdee et al, *The Public Law Outline: The Court Companion* (Family Law, 2008), for further discussion of the PLO.

The care plan and written agreements should bear in mind the welfare checklist, the Care Planning, Placement and Case Review (England) Regulations 2010, SI 2010/959, the *Framework for the Assessment of Children in Need and their Families* (DoH, 2000), *Assessing children in need and their families: Practice Guidance* (DoH, 2000) and LAC 99(29). See, also Chapter 7 (paras 7.1.1–7.1.4) and Chapter 16.

11.2.2 Checklist for basic initial information from medical witnesses

There is guidance in Part 25 of the FPR 2010 and the accompanying PD 25A as to the content of the letter of instruction to an expert and also the required content of an expert's report. See Chapter 18 for discussion of the instruction of experts, expert evidence and medical reports. In addition to this, the checklist below indicates the basic information which might be included in the report of a medical witness:

- Medical witness's full name.

- Health centre/surgery/hospital address/post held.

- Relevant qualifications and experience.

- Ensure that any opinions expressed are objective, relevant, and supported by observations.

- Nature, extent, venue and duration of examination(s) of the child:

    - date, duration and venue of first examination

    - reason for referral

    - observations of child on examination

    - appearance, demeanour, attitude to examination and others present

    - note any statements made by the child or by others that are relevant

    - any abnormalities in physical or mental state

    - marks, abrasions, wounds, skeletal survey, pain, tenderness

    - unusual features or appearance of any part of the body

- Body map showing location of areas of injury, bruising, etc. can be very helpful.

- Colour photographs are of great help to a court if the child/ family is willing to allow this, but beware, if sexual abuse is alleged, photography may remind child of the abuse or be further abusive.

- Description of the general health of the child.

- Full description of the child's injuries/abnormalities, with an explanation of the medical terms used.

- Is it possible to give a time of the occurrence of any injuries noted?

- When the injuries occurred, would they have caused pain to the child? Would he or she have cried out, screamed in pain? Does it still hurt? How soon afterwards would it stop hurting? Should a caring adult have noticed/treated the child's discomfort/pain?

- Were there attempts to treat the injuries/or to cover them up?

- Is there any evidence of brittle bones or other congenital factor likely to contribute to these injuries or explain them?

- If anyone was questioned about the injuries, note who was questioned, who was present, their reactions and demeanour in response to questioning, specific questions used, and responses given.

- Note any comments or explanations offered of how the injuries/abnormalities occurred.

- Does any explanation given by adults agree/conflict with the medical or psychiatric diagnosis?

- Describe diagnosis, treatment given or recommended following examination and prognosis.

- Note date(s), venue and duration of subsequent examinations.

- Record any other relevant or significant health issues within family (including parents, siblings, other relatives), particularly any issues affecting the parents' or carers' ability to look after the child, or affecting the general health and welfare of the child or close family members.

- Health history of the child, in chronological order, including:

  - physical development

  - height/weight/centile charts

  - developmental assessments according to age

  - visual/hearing/neurological/speech/language assessments

  - evidence of emotional problems/abnormalities (Have they been diagnosed as a congenital disorder, or is there possibly some other cause?)

  - evidence of physical problems/abnormalities (Do they constitute an illness or 'disability' within the meaning of the CA 1989? Have they been diagnosed as a congenital disorder, or is there possibly some other cause?)

  - treatment(s) given to the child and the effect of treatment

  - advice offered to the family/child about medical care and whether the advice was taken up and acted upon

- Up-to-date information about the child's development.

- Other information concerning the child's welfare that is relevant for the helping agencies and the court.

Medical witnesses should bear in mind the welfare checklist whilst writing their report. It is a useful reference concerning the best interests of the child shared by the court, the children's guardian and the professionals in the case.

The names and addresses of doctors and other health professionals who have been involved with the child/family, or to whom child the child has been referred for specialist treatment or examination should be included. They may be able to give additional relevant information.

A list of 'dates to avoid' should be included, that is, times when unavailable for court, conferences and meetings.

A report should end with a 'statement of truth' see PLO, paragraph 3.3(13) and PD 17A accompanying the FPR 2010, which sets out the form for the statement of truth.

11.3   Preparation of the case

Good advocacy is not just an ability to speak persuasively in court. It is mostly good preparation. A good grasp of the facts of the case, the issues and the relevant law will generate confidence when putting forward an argument or making a point. Research on an issue will assist an advocate to ask questions that are useful to the court. Effective child and family law advocates are non-adversarial in approach, willing to negotiate and, when in court, they are courteous, clear, concise and accurate, having read all the case documentation thoroughly before the hearing.

A sound knowledge of the relevant law and the rules of evidence and procedure is essential and it is also vitally important to keep up to date with changes. For essential reading and sources for wider reference, see Chapter 19.

When researching legal material on the internet, reliable sources should be relied upon. For example, UK government websites, such as the Department for Education website, etc. where there can be tracked changes shown in relation to changes to legislation.

Other useful websites are available in Chapter 20, para 20.3.

11.4   Burden of proof and standard of proof in child law cases

Generally, the person alleging a fact must prove it. In child protection, the burden of proof is with the local authority. The standard of proof the local authority must reach is on a balance of probability, that is 'it is more likely than not' that there is actual or a potential risk of significant harm to the child. Neither the seriousness of any allegations nor the seriousness of the consequences should make any difference to the standard of proof to be applied in determining the facts, see

Re B (Children) (Care Orders: Standard of Proof) [2008] UKHL 35, [2008] 2 FLR 141, HL. This ruling was subsequently applied in *Re S-B (Children)* [2009] UKSC 17. The Supreme Court also decided that there are particular benefits in some cases in identifying the perpetrator. For example, by doing so, identification will allow the parties to work with the parent, and other members of the family, on the basis of the judge's findings. Also, the children would in later life, know the truth about who injured them. This is further discussed in Chapter 7.

11.5 Special evidence rules in child law cases

Child law cases should be non-adversarial. The focus of the case is the welfare of the child. The rules of evidence in child protection differ from other areas of law. The CA 1989 encourages admission of actions affecting the child without these becoming the basis for prosecution. In wardship proceedings the strict rules of evidence do not apply, see Butler-Sloss LJ in *Re H (Minor), Re K (Minors) (Child Abuse: Evidence)* [1989] 2 FLR 313 at 332–33. The general rules of evidence in non-child law cases render certain evidence inadmissible, that is, that relating to character, hearsay and opinion. In child law cases this evidence is admissible, see Figure 4.

11.5.1 Character

In child law cases, consideration of the character of those who care for the child is vitally important and evidence of convictions, medical and psychiatric history are admissible.

11.5.2 Best evidence and hearsay

The hearsay rule provides that witnesses may only give an account of what they themselves actually experienced as evidence of the truth of the alleged event. If a witness tells the court what someone else said, the words quoted cannot be admitted as proof that the thing reported actually happened. If A tells the court that 'On 14 July 2000, B said, "C hit me"', under the hearsay rule, this statement proves only that on that day B was alive and able to speak; that B spoke to A and that A heard his words; but it is not sufficient to prove that C did in fact hit B. B personally would have to come and give evidence of the event.

Figure 4   Admissible evidence in care proceedings

ORAL EVIDENCE may be given by:		ANY WITNESS MAY PRODUCE ALL OR ANY OF THESE:	
The child ...	Provided that the court is satisfied on enquiry that they understand the duty to tell the truth.	Photographs	Provided produced by taker, who has unretouched negatives and can produce originals.
		Tape recordings	Provided shown to be original and not tampered with.
Any witness of fact	Hearsay rule not applicable in family proceedings. Witness may not give opinions.	X-rays	As photographs.
		Other objects	eg clothing, weapons, admissible provided relevant.
An expert witness	May give fact and opinion, can refer to charts, notes, tables and reference works.	Video recordings	If of an incident, admissible as photograph. Admissibility and content of interviews may be questioned.
Notes may be used provided that	They were made contemporaneously with events, or sufficiently soon thereafter for the memory of the person making the note to be clear.		

DOCUMENTARY EVIDENCE:

May be admissible provided it complies with s 1 Evidence Act 1938. Personal knowledge of facts or statement of fact is or forms part of continuous record in which the maker recorded facts given by another who had personal knowledge of them and maker gives evidence. Medical notes come into this category. Special rules for computer records. Copies may be accepted for same reason if certified to be true copies. Documents copied by the children's guardian may be adduced in evidence, s 42 CA 1989.

SELF-PRODUCING DOCUMENTS:

Memorandum of conviction	Admissible under s 7(2) of the Rehabilitation of Offenders Act 1974, Sched 13 of the Children Act 1989, and s 73 of the Police and Criminal Evidence Act 1984, and Home Office Circulars 88/1982; 105/1982; and 102/1988, and see Police Act 1997, Pt V.
School attendance records	Admissible under s 95 Education Act 1944.
Medical certificate	Admissible under s 26 CYPA 1963.

In child law cases, however, the court requires all relevant evidence, and, in certain circumstances, it admits hearsay. The wishes and feelings of children are important, and quotations from others about the child or of what the child said can be vital. Section 96(3) of the CA 1989, and the Children (Admissibility of Hearsay Evidence) Order 1993, SI 1993/621 provide that in civil proceedings before the High Court or a county court, family proceedings, and civil proceedings in a magistrates' court under the Child Support Act 1991, evidence given in connection with the upbringing, maintenance or welfare of a child shall be admissible notwithstanding any rule of law relating to hearsay. Family proceedings are defined in sections 8(3) and 105 of the CA 1989. Section 4 of the Civil Evidence Act 1995 contains helpful criteria in the assessment of hearsay evidence.

The court requires the originals of all notes produced, including those made contemporaneously, not just the neatly typed copies made subsequently. Notes should be written up at the time or as soon as possible after the event recorded. If notes are made days after an event, their reliability may be questioned. See, in particular, the case of *Re P (Children)* [2010] EWCA Civ 672, where the Court of Appeal decided that a generalised finding can be made against the respondent in a care case. The evidence in this case took the form of the foster carer's diary, which contained statements made by the child as to allegations of sexual abuse directed towards the respondent. The court was satisfied that the diary entries were an accurate record of statements made by the child.

11.5.3   Opinion

Witnesses may give factual or expert evidence. Witnesses of fact may not give their opinion and are expected to restrict themselves to a full and accurate account of what happened. The court draws inferences from the facts. Experts may draw inferences, and offer opinions based on the facts, research and their own learning and experience. They should behave in a professional manner, and be impartial, see Chapter 18.

11.5.4   Statements made by children's guardians

Under section 41(11)(a)–(b) of the CA 1989, the court may take account of any statement contained in the report of a children's guardian, and of any evidence given in respect of matters referred to in the guardian's report. The court has the power to regulate its own proceedings, and will assess the weight to give to such evidence. The children's guardian has access to (and may cite) local authority records, see section 42; and should draw to the attention of the court for directions any local authority papers which are relevant, but which the local authority does not intend to disclose, see *Re C (Expert Evidence: Disclosure: Practice)* [1995] 1 FLR 204.

See, in particular, PD 16A accompanying the FPR 2010. Paragraph 6.10 provides that where the children's guardian inspects records of the kinds referred to in: (a) section 42 of the CA 1989 (right to have access to local authority records); or (b) section 103 of the Adoption and Children Act 2002 (right to have access to adoption agency records), the children's guardian must bring all records and documents which may, in the opinion of the children's guardian, assist in the proper determination of the proceedings to the attention of: (i) the court; and (ii) unless the court directs otherwise, the other parties to the proceedings.

11.5.5 No professional privilege for medical or psychiatric reports

Medical records must be disclosed on production of a witness summons. There is a need for full and frank disclosure of material in all matters relating to children, because the welfare of the child is of paramount importance. This includes medical reports unfavourable to a client's interests, see *Essex CC v R (A Minor)* [1993] 2 FLR 826, and *Oxfordshire CC v M* [1994] 1 FLR 175, in which the Court of Appeal upheld this principle. Communications between lawyer and client remain privileged.

In relation to the issuing of a witness summons, rule 24.2 of the FPR 2010 provides for a witness summons to be issued by the court, requiring a witness to attend court to give evidence, or to produce documents to the court. The prescribed form is set out in PD 24A and PD5A accompanying the FPR 2010. If a person seeks to have a summons issued less than seven days before the date of the hearing, permission of the court is required.

Also note Article 13 of the Family Procedure (Modification of Enactments) Order 2011, SI 2011/1045, which amends the Magistrates' Courts Act 1980, so as to enable a magistrate, in family proceedings, to issue a witness summons.

11.5.6 Directions hearings – ordering the evidence

Delay must be avoided, section 1(2) of the CA 1989. Directions appointments enable the court to control the preparation of evidence and listing hearings.

Form PLP10 is an order menu, which contains a list of standard directions to be used in children law cases under the Private Law Programme.

In care cases, there are the various forms referred to in PD 12A and also PD 5A accompanying the FPR 2010. In particular, consider the local authority case summary (PLO3), the draft case management order (PLO4), the allocation record and timetable for the child (PLO5), the directions and allocation on issue of proceedings (PLO6), the directions and allocation at first appointment (PLO7), the standard directions on issue (PLO8) and the standard directions at first appointment (PLO9).

Permission of the court is required to withhold documents from a party, see the case of *A Local Authority v M & M (by their Guardian) & Ors* [2009] EWHC 3172 (Fam), where Hedley J considered withholding some of the documents from respondent father, and even providing for some documents to be redacted, but on the facts, took the more draconian step of discharging him as a party.

Where one party seeks to prevent another from seeing a document, an application should be made on notice and transferred to the High Court, *Re M (Disclosure)* [1998] 2 FLR 1028. The directions may also stipulate the venue of any assessments to be carried out, who should accompany the child and to whom the results should be given.

The court's permission is required for disclosure of documents to experts unless the instruction of the expert has been directed by the court, in which case documents can be released, see Part 25 of the FPR 2010 and the accompanying PD 25A and PD 12G.

Permission of the court is required for the disclosure of documents to a non-party, although see rules 12.70–12.75 of the FPR 2010 and the accompanying PD 12G, which allow communication of information in some limited cases.

Permission of the court is required for medical or psychiatric examinations or assessments of children, pursuant to section 38(6) and (7) of the CA 1989.

See also *Re X (Disclosure for the Purposes of Criminal Proceedings)* [2008] EWHC 242 (Fam), [2008] Fam Law 725 and *Re M (Case Disclosure to Police)* [2008] Fam Law 618, Baron J.

Expert witnesses are widely used, and advocates build up good working relationships with them. See Chapter 18 for instruction of experts, judicial guidance, how to find the right expert and resource issues. Before the directions hearing the advocate should ascertain whether experts are available, how long assessments will take, cost, legal aid and any assistance the experts may require. The expert should confirm availability, enabling the court to fix a suitable hearing date. See, in particular, Part 25 of the FPR 2010 and the accompanying PD 25A, which sets out the provisions surrounding instruction of experts in cases. Also see the Community Legal Service (Funding) (Amendment No 2) Order 2011, SI 2011/2066 (and watch for any subsequent amendments), which sets out, amongst other things, the rates of payment of expert services.

11.6 Court procedure at the hearing

Procedure is addressed separately in the chapters dealing with each order. However, hearings follow a reasonably consistent pattern common to most applications under the CA 1989.

11.6.1 Notes of evidence

Rule 23.9 of the FPR 2010 provides that in proceedings in a magistrates' court, the justices' clerk or the court shall keep a note of the substance of the oral evidence given at a directions appointment or at a hearing of any proceedings.

11.6.2 Order of evidence

Part 22 of the FPR 2010 sets out specific issues and requirements relevant to evidence.

In particular, rule 22.1 of the FPR 2010 provides for the court to control the evidence by giving directions as to:

- the issues on which it would seek evidence to be provided;

- the nature of the evidence which it requires, in order to decide the issues; and

- the way it was going to be placed before the court.

It is, therefore, very important for legal representatives to have a clear idea of which witnesses they would wish to attend court and why. For example, is that witness required for purposes of giving evidence on threshold, contact or disposal? It should always be ensured that consideration is given to whether the evidence of that witness can be agreed, in order to avoid that witness being called, in accordance with the overriding objective under Part 1 of the FPR 2010. Therefore, at the issues resolution hearing (the purpose of which is to narrow down the salient issues in the case, and even finalising the case), legal representatives should be prepared and clear about which witnesses are to be called and what they will go on to prove.

Rule 22.4 of the FPR 2010 sets out the format of a witness statement, and in particular that it needs to comply with the accompanying PD 22A. It must also contain a statement of truth, for the form see PLO, paragraph 3.3(13) and PD 17A.

Rule 22.1 of the FPR 2010 allows the court to exclude evidence that would otherwise be admissible and can limit the cross-examination (rule 22.4).

Unless the courts create a variation of procedure, the order of evidence in a care matter tends to be as follows:

(a)   applicant;

(b)   any party with parental responsibility for the child;

(c)   other respondents (including a child who is separately represented);

(d)   the children's guardian;

(e)   the child, if he is not a party and there is no children's guardian.

(This is a situation mainly relevant to private law cases, since in most cases under Part IV of the CA 1989 there is a children's guardian appointed and a child of sufficient age to instruct a lawyer separately will be a party.)

11.6.3   Extent of evidence

There are some limitations on the courts regulating their own proceedings. They must normally hear some evidence, even if the matter is agreed. It is not normally sufficient to file statements and to rely on these to support a case, calling no oral evidence at all, although this may occur in exceptional circumstances. In *Re B (Minors) (Contact)* [1994] 2 FLR 1 at 6A(1)–(6), Butler-Sloss LJ in the Court of Appeal, hearing an issue of defined contact, gave guidance to the courts on approaching the matter of how much evidence is appropriate.

In *Re F (Minor) (Care Order: Procedure)* [1994] 1 FLR 240 a magistrates' court which had heard evidence from the local authority but refused to hear the evidence of the father was held to be quite wrong. The justices should have heard the evidence from both sides. In *S v Merton LBC* [1994] 1 FCR 186, a family proceedings court (FPC) was criticised for making its decision on submissions only and it was held that some evidence at least is required. See Munby J on bundles in *Re X and Y (Court Bundles)* [2008] EWHC 2058 (Fam).

Consider rule 22.2 of the FPR 2010, which provides that generally, any fact which needs to be proved by the evidence of witnesses is to be proved: (a) at the final hearing, by their oral evidence; and (b) at any other hearing, by their evidence in writing. There is an exception to this rule, however, where it is stated that the general rule does not apply to applications under Part 12 for secure accommodation orders, interim care orders, interim supervision orders, or where an enactment provides otherwise. One particular example referred to is in the case of an application for a emergency protection order, whereby section 45(7) of the CA 1989 provides that the evidence may be take into account when the court is hearing an application.

11.6.4 Directions hearing checklist

* List of witnesses
* Dates to avoid (prior engagements of):
    - parties
    - witnesses of fact
    - expert witnesses
    - advocate
* Information and assistance for court proceedings:
    - reference material
    - exhibits
    - interpreter
    - visual aids in court
    - TV links; tape recorder/player
    - security

- – wheelchair access

- – hearing loop, etc.

- Information for expert witnesses:

  - – documents in case

  - – exhibits to be sent to expert or in expert's possession

  - – chronology

  - – arrangements for conference of experts

- Permission of the court or consents necessary:

  - – disclosure of documents, information, exhibits

  - – medical or psychiatric examinations and their venue, who will accompany child, to whom results are to be given

  - – bloods or other special testing (does it need High Court consent, e.g. HIV?)

  - – excuse party/child attendance at court

  - – accommodation of child

  - – withholding information from party (High Court consent)

- Statements and reports to be filed with the court:

  - – parties; witnesses; experts; chronology; reports; other

  - – documents from files Statements or reports late?

  - – consent of the court required for late filing

- Service:

  - – applicant and parties; those entitled to notice of the proceedings; those entitled to be respondents; children's guardian; others

11.7 Courtroom skills

11.7.1 Court manners

Proceedings are non-adversarial, and in an inevitably emotional situation, a calm advocate can assist everyone greatly in family proceedings. Forms of address are as follows:

Magistrates	Your Worship, Sir or Madam (usually pronounced Ma'am)
Deputy/District Judge	Sir or Madam (pronounced Ma'am)
Recorder	Your Honour
County Court Judge	Your Honour
High Court and Court of Appeal Judges	My Lord or My Lady (usually pronounced by the Bar as M' Lord or M' Lady)
Barristers and solicitors (referring to each other)	'My (learned) friend, Counsel for X or Mr, Mrs or Ms ...' etc.

Cases are listed on a notice outside the court room with the time of hearing. Children cases are often listed just by the court case reference number or otherwise anonymised, e.g. *Kent County Council v X.*

Greet other parties and advocates on arrival at court, letting the court usher know of your arrival. Ushers will enter the names of everyone present on their court list, noting who are the parties, advocates, and witnesses.

In court, stand while the judge or magistrates enter the room, and wait for them to be seated before sitting down yourself. Figure 5 illustrates a typical FPC courtroom layout and seating. The FPCs and county courts may conduct their proceedings seated. Check with the clerk to the court or the usher. The general rule is that advocates or witnesses should stand whilst speaking or when giving evidence, until invited to sit.

The applicant's advocate usually introduces other advocates and the parties to the court, or sometimes the judge or magistrate may invite people to introduce themselves. To be prepared, check the names of parties, other advocates and witnesses before going into court.

The task of an advocate is to present the facts and the law to the court and to put forward to the court their client's point of view in a reasoned and courteous manner. In children and family cases, questioning should be to elicit clarity and detail, and not be belligerent or adversarial. Advocates will therefore be asking questions of witnesses to clarify statements filed with the court or to elicit new information. A good tip for advocates is not to ask questions to which the answer is unknown (unless of course such a question is absolutely necessary), otherwise, in the answer, be prepared for surprises.

Do not interrupt another advocate or witness when they are addressing the court. Allow them to finish what they were saying, then request the court's permission to correct any factual or legal errors. Do not interrupt an advocate who is asking questions, wait, let the advocate finish and then speak.

Advise witnesses that, when giving evidence, they should turn slightly to face the bench, and maintain eye contact with the judge or the magistrates while addressing all answers to them (rather than looking back towards the advocate asking the questions). This is not only good court practice, but it also very effectively prevents advocates from interrupting the witness's evidence, as to do so would then seem discourteous to the judge or magistrates. If an over-enthusiastic or aggressive advocate interrupts before a witness has said all that they wanted to, advise the witness to turn to the judge or bench and say, politely, that before they answer the new question, they would first like to finish the point that they wanted to make in response to the original question.

Making audible comments or critical 'asides' in court to other advocates, parties or others is not acceptable, and is unprofessional.

Outside the courtroom, maintain quiet, professional courtesy to everyone. Remember that the parties are likely to be under stress and be aware of their feelings. Loud conversations between advocates discussing the case, comments about others, jokes, holiday memories and personal family/pet anecdotes are not professionally appropriate.

If a client wishes to say something to his or her advocate in the courtroom as the evidence unfolds, the client should do so quietly, and if it is necessary to have a longer conversation, an adjournment may be sought to take instructions.

Bring to court sufficient spare copies of documents and draft orders for the court and all the parties and witnesses who may need to have one. The original goes to the judge or bench, with a copy to the clerk. If there are magistrates, each should have a copy if possible.

The examination of witnesses follows the order of evidence. Each witness is called to the witness box, sworn in by the usher or by the clerk of the court (or requested to affirm) and then examined in chief. Questions which suggest an answer are 'leading questions' and forbidden in examination in chief; one must not 'lead the witness'. For example, ask 'What time of day was it when ...?' not 'Was it three o'clock when ...?'.

Figure 5 Layout of typical family proceedings court

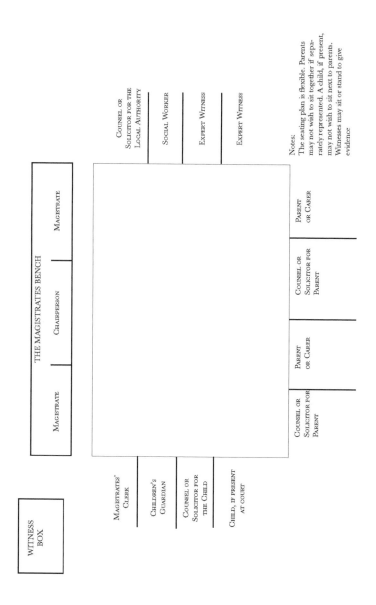

THE MAGISTRATES BENCH

MAGISTRATE · CHAIRPERSON · MAGISTRATE

WITNESS BOX

MAGISTRATES' CLERK

CHILDREN'S GUARDIAN

COUNSEL OR SOLICITOR FOR THE CHILD

CHILD, IF PRESENT AT COURT

COUNSEL OR SOLICITOR FOR THE LOCAL AUTHORITY

SOCIAL WORKER

EXPERT WITNESS

EXPERT WITNESS

COUNSEL OR SOLICITOR FOR PARENT

PARENT OR CARER

COUNSEL OR SOLICITOR FOR PARENT

PARENT OR CARER

Notes:
The seating plan is flexible. Parents may not wish to sit together if separately represented. A child, if present, may not wish to sit next to parents. Witnesses may sit or stand to give evidence

The other parties may then cross-examine the witness, for example to clarify issues or to check facts, and the party calling the witness may re-examine to clarify points already made. One may not usually raise new evidence in re-examination unless with the permission of the court. The court should then be offered the opportunity to ask any questions of the witness that it wishes. If the witness is not likely to be required further, permission of the court is required to discharge the witness before he or she leaves the court. Some witnesses, particularly experts, may be asked to remain either in court, on the premises or 'on call' in case they are needed again.

Traditionally, the applicant opens the case and outlines his or her case to the court. The other parties then have the opportunity to make a speech to the court but they will usually do so at the end of the case. The children's guardian or the child's advocate will be the last to speak. If there are submissions on law during the case, the order of address follows the order of evidence.

When the case is completed, the court should stand for the magistrates or judge to leave the room.

These notes are necessarily brief, but there are many good books and courses on advocacy. By far the best way of learning courtroom skills is to sit in on cases (with the permission of the court and the parties) alongside experienced Children Panel advocates to learn by observation – not necessarily to copy their style. Each of us will, over time and with practice, develop our own individual strengths and skills as advocates or become efficient and cogent professional witnesses.

12 Children's Rights

The law affecting the rights of children includes the Children Act 1989 (CA 1989), the UN Convention on the Rights of the Child (UNCRC) (ratified by the UK in 1991) and the Human Rights Act 1998 (in force in the UK from 2 October 2000), which incorporates the European Convention for the Protection of Human Rights and Fundamental Freedoms 1950 (ECHR) and its Protocols into UK law. Other legislation affords specific rights to children and families, for example in mental health, and is cited below where relevant.

Under section 22(4) of the Human Rights Act 1998, all proceedings brought by a public authority are subject to the ECHR, even where the alleged breach of these rights occurred before the coming into force of the Act.

12.1 To accept or refuse medical treatment

No adult or child competent to make their own medical decisions may be given medical treatment without their consent. Treatment without consent (save in emergencies) may incur liability for damages for assault, or constitute an offence in criminal law. Detention in hospital or any other place without consent could constitute false imprisonment.

It is important to make a clear distinction between two situations in which consent may be required. The first is where doctors seek to carry out diagnostic assessments which may be necessary before deciding on the best method of treatment, and/or medical, psychiatric or psychological treatments necessary to maintain the child's health and welfare. The second category is where medical, psychiatric or psychological assessments are sought for purely forensic purposes.

Depending on the child's age and other considerations, in special circumstances the courts may overrule a child's refusal of necessary treatment, but the courts will be far less willing to overrule a child's refusal of an assessment for forensic purposes.

The issue, therefore, is at what age can a child give valid consent?

12.1.1   Children over 16 (but under 18)

Under section 8 of the Family Law Reform Act 1969, at the age of 16, a young person gains the right to give informed consent to surgical, medical or dental treatment. Examinations or assessments must impliedly be included. The consent of the young person is as valid as that of an adult. A young person with mental illness, disability or psychiatric disturbance may be subject to the Mental Health Act 1983.

If a young person consents to recommended medical or dental treatment, therefore (even if his or her parents disagreed for some reason), the medical or dental practitioner would be protected from a claim for damages for trespass to the person.

However, if the young person refuses recommended treatment – although those with parental responsibility for the young person may give a valid consent which will have the effect of protecting the medical or dental practitioner from claims for damages for trespass to the person – it should be noted that as the age of the young person increases towards 18, his or her refusal and the reasons for it are important considerations for parents and the court.

In the event of a dispute about consent for medical treatment, the issue should be taken before the High Court, either under its inherent jurisdiction or under section 8 of the CA 1989 for a specific issue order. In the case of *Re W (A Minor) (Consent to Medical Treatment)* [1993] 1 FLR 1 the Court of Appeal gave consent for the treatment of a girl of 16 with anorexia nervosa, despite her refusal.

In circumstances requiring sterilisation, termination of a pregnancy or surgical interventions to save or prolong the child's life, if the child is a ward of court, the High Court's consent is required.

If parents refuse to allow medical treatment and the child needs it, the High Court can provide the requisite authority under its inherent jurisdiction.

Changes made to section 131 of the Mental Health Act 1983 by section 43 of the Mental Health Act 2007 mean that when a young person of 16 or 17 has capacity (as defined in the Mental Capacity Act 2005) and does not consent to admission for treatment for mental disorder (because he or she is overwhelmed, does not want to consent or refuses to consent), he or she cannot then be admitted informally on the basis of the consent of a person with parental responsibility (see chapter 36 of the Code of Practice to the Mental Health Act 1983, as amended in 2008).

12.1.2   Children under 16

The legal situation for consent by children under 16 but who are judged to be '*Gillick* competent' is similar to that of young people over 16, described in para 12.1.1. For those who are not considered to be '*Gillick* competent', decisions concerning medical treatment are made for them by those with parental responsibility and, where necessary, the courts will intervene or assist in the ways described above.

In *Gillick v West Norfolk and Wisbech AHA* [1986] AC 112 the House of Lords formulated the concept now known colloquially as '*Gillick* competence' in which the ability of a child under 16 to make her own medical decisions is evaluated according to chronological age considered in conjunction with the child's mental and emotional maturity, intelligence and comprehension.

Lord Scarman made it clear in the *Gillick* case that:

> It will be a question of fact whether a child seeking advice has sufficient understanding of what is involved to give a consent valid in law. Until the child achieves the capacity to consent, the parental right to make the decision continues save only in exceptional circumstances. Emergency, parental neglect, abandonment of the child, or inability to find the parent are examples of exceptional situations.

'*Gillick* competence' has been reviewed in a number of subsequent cases. The most notable recent case was *R (Axon) v Secretary of State for Health* [2006] EWHC 37 (Admin), in which a mother challenged through judicial review the Department of Health guidance for confidentiality on the issue of the provision of abortion for her daughter aged 15, without the mother's knowledge. The court held that the *Gillick* decision remained authoritative as to the lawfulness of the provision by health care professionals of confidential advice and treatment to young people under 16, without parental knowledge or consent. The *Gillick* guidelines must, however, be strictly observed.

In *Re S (Minor) (Refusal of Treatment)* [1995] 1 FCR 604 it was held that a girl of almost 16 suffering from thalassaemia major should continue with her treatment, despite her refusal to do so on religious grounds. The discontinuance of treatment would have resulted in her death within a few weeks. The court acknowledged that at 18 she could refuse and effectively end her life, but expressed the hope that in the intervening period she might change her mind or that gene therapy would relieve her condition.

See also *Re L (Medical Treatment: Gillick Competency)* [1998] 2 FLR 810 and *Re M (Child: Refusal of Medical Treatment)* [1999] 2 FCR 577, where a heart transplant was authorised for a 15-year-old girl.

Understanding the potential consequences of refusing treatment or assessment increases with the child's age, maturity, intelligence and level of understanding, influenced by the detail of the information provided. The *Reference guide to consent for examination or treatment* (DoH, 2nd edn, 2009), pp 32–38 should be consulted.

Where a child under the age of 16 lacks capacity to consent (i.e. is not '*Gillick* competent'), consent may be given on the child's behalf by any one person with parental responsibility (if the matter is within the 'zone of parental control' as defined by the Mental Health Act 1983) or by the court. Those giving consent on behalf of child patients must have the capacity to consent to the intervention in question, be acting voluntarily and be appropriately informed. The power to consent must be exercised according to the welfare principle (section 1 of the CA 1989): that the child's welfare must be paramount. Even where a child lacks capacity to consent on his or her own behalf, it is good practice to involve the child as much as possible in the decision-making process.

Where necessary, the courts have power to overrule the refusal by a person with parental responsibility for any necessary mental or medical assessment and/or treatment of a child. Certain important decisions, such as sterilisation for contraceptive purposes, should be referred to the courts for guidance, even if those with parental responsibility have given consent for the operation.

For medical and psychiatric treatment in the context of supervision orders, see para 12.2.1.

12.1.3   Mentally disordered children

Where a child is mentally ill or mentally disordered and unable to make a legally valid decision for himself, the High Court in its wardship jurisdiction may consent on behalf of a person under 18. The High Court may order reasonable force to be used to ensure compliance, see *A Metropolitan Borough Council v DB* [1997] 1 FLR 767, where the court held that a hospital was 'secure' within the meaning of section 25 of the CA 1989.

12.1.4   Where no one has parental responsibility

In situations where an immediate decision or action is needed and no one with parental responsibility is available, section 3(5) of the CA 1989 provides:

a person who:

(a) does not have parental responsibility for a particular child; but

(b) has care of the child,

may ... do what is reasonable in all the circumstances of the case for the purpose of safeguarding or promoting the child's welfare.

This section is intended for use by neighbours, relatives or others, such as foster carers, looking after children who may need to take the child urgently to the GP or dentist, but should not be used to give consent for major medical decisions.

12.2 To accept or refuse medical or psychiatric assessment

Child protection often necessitates medical or psychiatric examination or assessment. The *Report of the Inquiry into Child Abuse in Cleveland* (HMSO, 1987) demonstrated that repeated medical examinations can themselves be abusive. The court has wide power to set limits by directions, for example, the place and time of an examination, person(s) to be present, person(s) to conduct the examination and person(s) or authorities to whom the results shall be given.

12.2.1 Circumstances in which the court may direct medical or psychiatric examination or assessment which the child has a right to refuse

In the following circumstances, a child of sufficient understanding has the right to refuse consent to medical or psychiatric examination:

(a) interim care order, section 38(6) of the CA 1989;

(b) interim supervision order, section 38(6);

(c) emergency protection order, section 44(6)(b) and (7);

(d) child assessment order, section 43(8).

In supervision orders, the child may be directed to undergo a medical, but not a psychiatric examination, but (where the child has sufficient understanding to exercise their right of consent) the court may only make this direction if the child consents, see Schedule 3, paragraph 4 to the CA 1989. The court may order psychiatric or medical treatment of a child under a supervision order in specified circumstances and consent is required of a child who has sufficient understanding to exercise his or her right of consent, see Schedule 3, paragraph 5.

Where the child has the right to refuse medical or psychiatric examinations, his wishes and feelings must be ascertained by the children's guardian, or doctor, see *The Children Act 1989 Guidance and Regulations* (DCSF), Volume 1 *Court Orders*, paragraph 3.52.

Doctors must check whether the child is capable of giving an informed decision, and that he consents, before proceeding with an examination. Even if the court has directed an examination with the child's consent, if, when the child is with the doctor he then refuses, the doctor should not proceed, but should refer the matter back to the court. If the court agrees that this is an informed decision, then usually the court will respect the refusal, but if the refusal may place the child in serious danger, then it is possible that the High Court may overrule the refusal in the child's best interests. Such an event would be rare.

12.3 To make his or her own application to the court

Under section 10(8) of the CA 1989, children of sufficient age and understanding may make their own applications for section 8 orders, with leave of the court.

Following *Re SC (Minor) (Leave to Seek Residence Order)* [1994] 1 FLR 96, where the child is the applicant, his welfare is paramount because the provisions of section 10(9) of the CA 1989 do not apply. (Section 10(9) sets out the criteria for the court's consideration in granting leave for all other applicants, and it has been held that the child's welfare is not paramount in those applications.) Also, everyone with parental responsibility for the child should have notice of the application (see Chapter 13, para 13.2.2).

Children may seek other orders under the CA 1989, with leave, including discharge of:

* care;

* supervision;

* emergency protection;

* section 8 orders;

* parental responsibility orders;

* parental responsibility agreements.

The decision as to whether a child is of sufficient age and understanding to apply is a matter initially for the solicitor instructed by the child, but ultimately for the court to decide *Re CT (Minor)*

(Wardship: Representation) [1993] 3 WLR 602, [1993] 2 FLR 278. The court can appoint a children's guardian for the child under rule 16.4 of the FPR 2010 or a litigation friend, usually the Official Solicitor, under rules 16.5–16.16 and the accompanying PD 16.

12.4 To request confidentiality and, in the event of disagreement with the children's guardian, to instruct a solicitor separately

Where a child is subject to care or supervision applications, the child has a solicitor appointed for him or her by the children's guardian or the court. The child's solicitor takes instructions from the children's guardian and from the child. A child of sufficient age and understanding may request client confidentiality with his or her solicitor on specific issues or generally.

A child of sufficient age and understanding may disagree with the recommendations of the children's guardian, remaining a party with his own solicitor. The guardian will notify the court and continue unrepresented or appoint another solicitor. Procedure is governed by rule 16.29(2)–(3) of the FPR 2010. The ethics, duties and responsibilities of the solicitor for the child are discussed in Chapter 15.

12.5 Rights of a child in care

Rights of children who are looked after by the local authority are covered in Chapter 7.

12.6 UN Convention on the Rights of the Child

The UNCRC has been ratified by the UK government but is not incorporated into UK law. This means that it is persuasive on the courts rather than binding in the same way as the ECHR. Article 12 of the UNCRC states that children who are capable of forming their own views have a right to express these in matters affecting them and to have due weight placed on their views in accordance with their age and maturity, in particular, to be heard in any judicial or administrative proceedings affecting them. This Article is increasingly cited in the courts as reflecting awareness of taking young people's own views into account, for example, *Mabon v Mabon* [2005] EWCA Civ 634.

13 Other Orders available to the Court in Family Proceedings

The Children Act 1989 (CA 1989) empowers the court to make certain orders of its own volition in 'family proceedings', defined in section 8(3) and as including Parts I, II and III; the Matrimonial Causes Act 1973; the Family Law Act 1996; the Adoption and Children Act 2002; and others. There is a menu of orders available in family proceedings (see Figure 6) from which the court may choose, subject to the principles of section 1 of the CA 1989. Note that the court should make no order unless it is necessary for the welfare of the child, see Chapter 2. The court cannot, however, intervene in family proceedings to impose orders for care, supervision, secure accommodation, emergency protection or child assessment.

13.1 Orders in family proceedings

Family assistance orders require no application, but the parties must agree to their making. Special guardianship orders may be made of the court's own volition, but require the consent of the person in whose favour it is made, see Chapter 10. Note also that in the magistrates' court, unlike the other courts, all proceedings under CA 1989 are classed as family proceedings under section 92(2).

13.2 Section 8 orders

Section 8(1) of the CA 1989 creates the section 8 orders: contact, prohibited steps, residence and specific issue, all available in all family proceedings. The court may regulate, on an application or of its own volition, the child's residence and contact with others; prohibit specified steps without leave of the court; and deal with any specific issues arising in the child's upbringing.

Figure 6   Menu of orders available in family proceedings

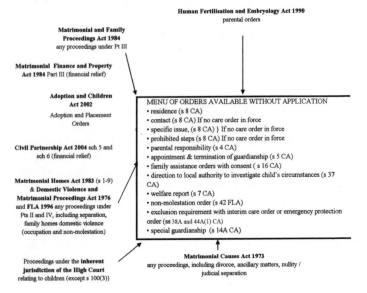

THE PROCEEDINGS SET OUT AROUND THE BOX ARE 'FAMILY
PROCEEDINGS' AS DEFINED IN S 8 (4) CA 1989

Human Fertilisation and Embryology Act 1990
parental orders

**Matrimonial and Family
Proceedings Act 1984**
any proceedings under Pt III

**Matrimonial Finance and Property
Act 1984** Part III (financial relief)

**Adoption and Children
Act 2002**
Adoption and Placement
Orders

Civil Partnership Act 2004 sch 5 and
sch 6 (financial relief)

Matrimonial Homes Act 1983 (s 1-9)
**& Domestic Violence and
Matrimonial Proceedings Act 1976**
and FLA 1996 any proceedings under
Pts II and IV, including separation,
family homes domestic violence
(occupation and non-molestation)

MENU OF ORDERS AVAILABLE WITHOUT APPLICATION
• residence (s 8 CA)
• contact (s 8 CA) If no care order in force
• specific issue, (s 8 CA) } If no care order in force
• prohibited steps (s 8 CA) If no care order in force
• parental responsibility (s 4 CA)
• appointment & termination of guardianship (s 5 CA)
• family assistance orders with consent (s 16 CA)
• direction to local authority to investigate child's circumstances (s 37
CA)
• welfare report (s 7 CA)
• non-molestation order (s 42 FLA)
• exclusion requirement with interim care order or emergency protection
order (ss 38A and 44A(1) CA)
• special guardianship (s 14A CA)

Proceedings under the **inherent
jurisdiction of the High Court**
relating to children (except s 100(3))

Matrimonial Causes Act 1973
any proceedings, including divorce, ancillary matters, nullity /
judicial separation

KEY
FLA = Family Law Act 1996
CA = Children Act 1989
CDA = Crime and Disorder Act 1998

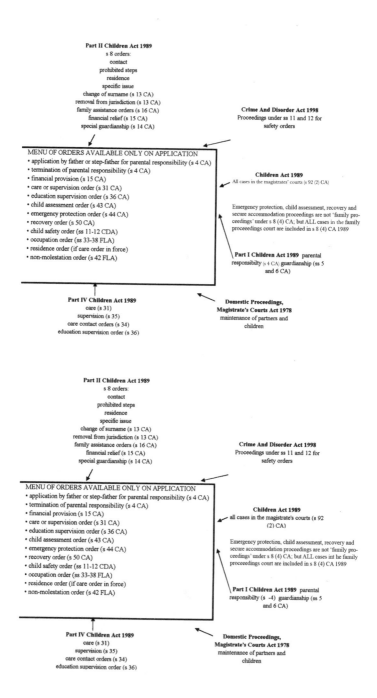

Some applicants are entitled to apply, and others must first seek the leave of the court. The following are entitled under section 10 of the CA 1989 to apply for any section 8 order:

(a) any parent or guardian of a child, section 10(4)(a) (this will include the unmarried father of a child whether or not he has parental responsibility);

(b) any person in whose favour a residence order is in force with respect to the child, section 10(4)(b). The following are entitled to apply for a residence or contact order (but not a prohibited steps order or a specific issue order):

    (i) any party to a marriage (whether or not subsisting) in relation to whom the child is a child of the family, section 10(5)(a) (this provision enables a step-parent to seek a residence or contact order);

    (ii) any person with whom the child has lived for a period of at least three years, section 10(5)(b) (s 10(10) provides that the three-year period need not be continuous but must have begun not more than five years before, or ended more than three months before, the making of the application);

13.2.1   Leave to apply

Any other person needs leave to apply for an order under section 8 of the CA 1989, including the child. An application by a child must be made to the county court (paragraph 6 of the Allocation and Transfer of Proceedings Order 2008, SI 2008/28). The court must be satisfied that a child applicant has sufficient understanding to make the proposed application, section 10(8) of the CA 1989. PD 16A accompanying the FPR 2010 sets out matters which the court will take into consideration when deciding if it is the child's best interests to be made a party under rule 16.2. An application for a residence order in respect of a child who is subject to a care order, if successful, would have the effect of discharging the care order.

Note that in *Re A (Care: Discharge Application by a Child)* [1995] 1 FLR 599, Thorpe J held that a child's application to discharge care was not one which required leave of the court.

13.2.2   Considerations on application for leave

Where the person applying for leave is not the child, section 10(9) of the CA 1989 applies. This requires that on applications for leave the court should have regard to various considerations which do not include the paramountcy principle. On the issue of leave, the welfare of the child is not of paramount importance because an application for leave is not a trial of the substantive issue, see *North Yorkshire CC v G* [1993] 2 FLR 732.

Section 10(9) of the CA 1989 sets out the matters to be taken into account:

(a)   the nature of the proposed application;

(b)   the applicant's connection with the child;

(c)   any risk that there might be of that proposed application disrupting the child's life to such an extent that he would be harmed by it; and

(d)   where the child is being looked after by a local authority:

    (i)   the authority's plans for the child's future; and

    (ii)   the wishes and feelings of the child's parents.

13.2.3   Duration

Other than residence orders, orders under section 8 of the CA 1989 subsist until the child reaches 16, unless they are brought to an end earlier by the court or made of limited duration, section 91(11). They may in exceptional circumstances be extended until the child reaches 18, section 9(6). Residence orders subsist until the child is 18, unless ended by the court. There is no such animal under the CA 1989 as an 'interim section 8 order' but instead, only a full order of limited duration, see *S v S (Custody Jurisdiction)* [1995] 1 FLR 155 and also *Re M (Official Solicitor's Role)* [1998] 2 FLR 815.

13.2.4   When the court may not make an order under section 8 of the Children Act 1989

(a)   Section 9(1) of the CA 1989 establishes restrictions on making section 8 orders:

    (i)   No court shall make any order under section 8 of the CA 1989, other than a residence order, with respect to a child who is in the care of a local authority.

    (ii)   A residence order will result in the automatic discharge of the care order, section 91(1) of the CA 1989. A care order automatically discharges a section 8 order, section 91(2).

(b)   Section 9(2) of the CA 1989 states: 'No application may be made by a local authority for a residence order or contact order and no court shall make such an order in favour of a local authority'.

(c)   Section 9(3) of the CA 1989 imposes restrictions on the application to the court for leave to apply for section 8 orders by some foster carers. All foster carers need leave of the court to apply for a section 8 order unless they are entitled to apply. If they have fostered the child within the preceding six months they will need the consent of the local authority before seeking leave to apply unless they are related to the child or the child has lived with them for at least one year preceding the application.

(d)   Section 9(4) of the CA 1989 goes on to provide that 'the period of three years ... need not be continuous, but must have begun not more than five years before the making of the application'.

(e)   Section 9(5)(a) of the CA 1989 forbids a court to make a specific issue or prohibited steps order 'with a view to achieving a result which could be achieved by making a residence or contact order'. Specific issue and prohibited steps orders are regarded as quite formidable powers, to be used sparingly and only where appropriate:

   (i)   Section 9(5)(b) of the CA 1989 forbids a court to exercise its power to make a specific issue or prohibited steps order 'in any way which is denied to the High Court (by section 100(2)) in the exercise of its inherent jurisdiction with respect to children'.

   (ii)   The essential purpose of section 100(2) of the CA 1989 is to ensure that local authorities seeking some measure of control over a child do so by way of proceedings under Part IV or Part V and not by invoking wardship. Section 9(5)(b) applies the same principle to section 8 proceedings.

   (iii)   Section 9(6) of the CA 1989 prohibits the making of any section 8 order which is to have effect for a period which will end after the child has reached the age of 16, unless the circumstances are exceptional. An application in respect of a child with severe learning difficulties or physical mobility problems may well constitute an exception.

13.2.5 Welfare reports in applications under section 8 of the Children Act 1989

Under section 7 of the CA 1989, the court may, when considering any question under the Act, ask for a report on the welfare of the child. The court may direct that a report be prepared by a Children and Family Court Advisory and Support Service (CAFCASS) officer or by a local authority. This refers to the court's power to direct CAFCASS to provide a report to assist its decision making in a section 8 application. In practice, CAFCASS officers may now work with parents toward dispute resolution without a report being written, see PD 12B accompanying the FPR 2010. A section 7 direction should be made to a local authority only where the family is already known to the authority.

13.3 Contact

In private law proceedings, a contact order made under section 8 of the CA 1989 means an order requiring the person with whom a child lives or is to live, to allow the child to visit the person named in the order, or for that person and the child otherwise to have contact with each other.

This order governs contact by direct and indirect means, including visits, staying over, telephone calls, tapes, videos, letters, cards and presents.

Contact orders generally will expire when the child reaches 16, unless there are exceptional circumstances, section 9(6) of the CA 1989.

Contact orders lapse if the parents live continuously together for more than six months, section 11(6) of the CA 1989.

13.3.1 Contact disputes

Children in private law disputes often find themselves caught up in bitter arguments between their parents about the arrangements for contact. This has the potential to cause children significant harm over time, and is often very difficult to manage. Contact orders are not always successful and do not deal with the underlying conflict which often results in allegations and counter allegations, and in the undermining or more obvious prevention of contact visits by a resident parent.

The court has the option to use contact activity orders (see para 13.3.2) to try to break these deadlocked cases; however, ultimately, it is only a change in the behaviour and attitude of parents that will result in a reduction of the conflict in such situations.

In some circumstances the court will order supervised contact within private law proceedings. Contact centres can provide a useful facility for the supervision of contact, but not all cases are suitable for such an arrangement.

This then leaves one-to-one supervision as the other alternative option. If there are no friends or family considered to be sufficiently neutral to provide this then a professional contact supervisor will be required. This results in one of the parties having to finance this arrangement as there is no other means available to facilitate the funding of such arrangements. For non-resident parents on a low income this will limit the amount of contact available to them as a direct result of their lack of resources. This is a very worrying development that has arisen as a direct consequence of the current climate of cutbacks to statutory agencies and is a situation that actively discriminates against the less well off in society.

Ultimately, it remains our view (Mitchels and James) that the most effective means of dealing with conflicted and intractable contact cases is through the use of a structured intervention combining supportive therapeutic and mediation techniques, allowing parents to explore and deal with the real issues underpinning the conflicted situation and to focus on meeting the needs and interests of the child, in a safe and contained manner.

13.3.2   Contact activity orders

Sections 11A–P were added to the CA 1989 by the Children and Adoption Act 2006 and are intended to facilitate and enforce contact orders where there is hostility between parties. They set out provisions for contact activity directions (sections 11A–B and E–F); contact activity conditions (sections 11C–F); monitoring contact (sections 11G–H); enforcement (sections 11I–N); and compensating for financial loss (sections 11O–P). Contact activities relate to referrals to services and programmes which are designed to promote safe contact, such as counselling or anger management. These facilitation and enforcement provisions seem to have been rarely used so far, the courts instead tending to rely on PD 12B accompanying the FPR 2010. Under paragraph 2(2), consideration and discussion of issues in section 8 applications will not take place until the first hearing dispute resolution appointment (FHDRA), apart from prior safety checks and enquiries carried out by CAFCASS before the first hearing.

At the FHDRA the court considers in particular:

(a) Whether and the extent to which the parties can safely resolve some or all of the issues with the assistance of the CAFCASS officer and any available mediator.

(b) Risk identification followed by active case management, including risk assessment and compliance with the *Practice Direction, Residence and Contact Orders: Domestic Violence and Harm*, 14 January 2009.

(c) Further dispute resolution.

(d) The avoidance of delay through the early identification of issues and timetabling, subject to the allocation order.

(e) Judicial scrutiny of the appropriateness of consent orders.

(f) Judicial consideration of the way to involve the child.

(g) Judicial continuity.

13.4 Prohibited steps

A prohibited steps order means an order that no step which could be taken by a parent in meeting his parental responsibility for a child, and which is of a kind specified in the order, shall be taken by any person without the consent of the court. This order enables the court to spell out those matters which are to be referred back to it for a decision. An example is an application to stop a child being known by a different surname, as in *Dawson v Wearmouth* [1999] 1 FLR 1167.

13.5 Residence

A residence order means an order settling the arrangements to be made as to the person with whom the child is to live. A 'shared residence order' refers to a residence order under section 11(4) of the CA 1989 made in favour of two people who do not live together, where the child spends a substantial amount of time in each household, for example *Re K (Shared Residence Order)* [2008] EWCA Civ 526, [2008] 2 FLR 380.

The court may make conditions and directions if necessary to facilitate the implementation of any order made under section 8 of the CA 1989.

13.5.1   Residence orders and parental responsibility

Residence orders do not remove parental responsibility from anyone else who has it. Parental responsibility can be given to the person in whose favour a residence order is made, remaining while the order is in force, section 12(2) of the CA 1989, and see Chapter 3. Residence orders generally expire when the child reaches 18, see para 13.2.3.

Section 12(1) of the CA 1989 specifically requires the court to make an order under section 4 giving parental responsibility to a father in favour of whom it makes a residence order if he would not otherwise have it. The court may not bring that parental responsibility order to an end while the residence order remains in force, section 12(4). There is an additional effect of the combined operation of section 12(2) and (4) for an unmarried father, which is that discharge of the residence order, or its expiry by effluxion of time, will not automatically result in the discharge of his parental responsibility for his child. He continues by implication to have parental responsibility for his child until the child reaches 18, unless it is specifically discharged by court order under section 4(4).

The CA 1989 does not allow parental responsibility given under this section to cover agreement to adoption, or an application under section 18 of the Adoption Act 1976, nor does it permit the appointment of a guardian for the child, section 12(3) of the CA 1989.

Section 13(1)(b) of the CA 1989 generally prohibits the removal of a child from the UK without the written consent of every person who has parental responsibility for the child or the leave of the court, whilst section 13(2) makes an exception permitting a person in whose favour a residence order is made to take the child abroad for a period of less than one month.

A parent who fears that a child may be removed abroad permanently on the pretext of a short holiday may apply for a prohibited steps order excluding the effect of section 13(2) of the CA 1989. Where the question of the removal of the child from the jurisdiction is anticipated the court may on the making of a residence order give leave either generally, or for specified purposes, section 13(3).

Where a child is subject to a residence order or to a care order, no person may change that child's surname without the written consent of every person with parental responsibility for that child, or leave of the court, section 13(1)(a) of the CA 1989. See *Re A (A Child: Joint Residence/Parental Responsibility)* [2008] EWHC Civ 867.

13.6 Specific issue

A specific issue order means an order giving directions for the purpose of determining a specific issue which has arisen, or which may arise, in connection with any aspect of parental responsibility for a child. Examples include medical vaccination or investigations, as in *Re C (A Child) (HIV Test)* [1999] 2 FLR 1004.

This order enables either parent to submit a particular dispute to the court for resolution in accordance with the child's best interests. The order was not envisaged as a way of giving one parent the right to determine issues in advance, nor was it intended to be a substitute for a residence or contact order.

Applications for contact orders, specific issue or prohibited steps orders cannot be made in respect of children subject to care orders, section 9(1) of the CA 1989.

13.7 Supplementary provisions

Section 11(1) of the CA 1989 instructs the court to 'draw up a timetable with a view to determining the question without delay' and 'to give such directions as it considers appropriate for the purpose of ensuring, so far as is reasonably practicable, that the timetable is adhered to'.

Section 11(2) of the CA 1989 permits rules of court to 'specify periods within which specified steps must be taken in relation to proceedings in which such questions arise' and 'to make other provision ... for the purpose of ensuring, so far as is reasonably practicable, that such questions are determined without delay', see the Family Procedure Rules 2010, SI 2010/2955 (FPR 2010).

Section 11(3) of the CA 1989 states that where a court has power to make a section 8 order, it may do so at any time in the course of the proceedings in question, even though it is not in a position to dispose finally of those proceedings.

Where a residence order is made in favour of two or more persons who do not themselves live together, the order may specify the periods during which the child is to live in the different households concerned, section 11(4) of the CA 1989.

Where there is a residence order in force, as a result of which the child lives, or is to live, with one of two parents who each have parental responsibility for him, the residence order shall cease to have effect if the parents live together for a continuous period of more than six months, section 11(5) of the CA 1989.

Section 11(6) of the CA 1989 states that, 'A contact order which requires the parent with whom a child lives to allow the child to visit, or otherwise have contact with, his other parent shall cease to have effect if the parents live together for a continuous period of more than six months'.

Orders made under section 8 of the CA 1989 orders may contain directions, impose conditions, be made for a specified period or contain provisions for a specified period; and make such incidental, supplemental or consequential provisions as the court thinks fit, section 11(7).

13.8   Practice and procedure in applications under section 8 of the Children Act 1989

Procedure is governed by Part 12 of the FPR 2010.

13.8.1   Applications

Freestanding applications should be on form C100 and, where applicable, form C1A or on form C2 if the application is made in existing 'family proceedings'. Form C1A should be added if there are any risks to parties or children identified in form C100.

If the application is for leave only, then, unless it is made without notice (see Chapter 18), the applicant for leave must complete form C2 giving reasons for the application and requesting leave in writing, and to file and serve the request together with the draft of the application on form C1 to each respondent, see Part 6, Chapter 3 of the FPR 2010.

13.8.2   Venue

Applications are made to the family proceedings court (FPC) or a county court family hearing centre, in accordance with the Allocation and Transfer of Proceedings Order 2008, SI 2008/28 which governs venue of hearings.

It is expected that applications under section 8 of the CA 1989 should be made at FPC level unless factors analogous with those that require transfer to county court or High Court level apply, see paragraph 15 of the Allocation and Transfer of Proceedings Order 2008 and Chapter 14.

13.8.3　Notice of application for orders under section 8 of the Children Act 1989

Under PD 12C accompanying the FPR 2010, notice shall be served on:

(a)　any local authority providing accommodation for the child;

(b)　persons who were caring for the child when proceedings commence;

(c)　any person providing refuge in which child is staying;

(d)　any person who the applicant believes is named in court order, still in effect, relating to child;

(e)　any party who the applicant believes is a party to pending proceedings relating to the child;

(f)　every person with whom the applicant believes the child has lived for three years prior to the application.

Notice of the proceedings is on form C6A, giving the date, time and venue of the hearing. It should be served at least 14 days before the hearing, PD 12C, paragraph 2.1 accompanying the FPR 2010.

13.8.4　Respondents

Under rule 12.3 of the FPR 2010, the following are automatically respondents to an application under section 8 of the CA 1989:

(a)　everyone with parental responsibility for the child;

(b)　if a care order is in force, everyone with parental responsibility when the order was made;

(c)　parties to proceedings leading to an order for which variation or discharge is now sought.

Respondents should be served with a copy of the application with the date of hearing endorsed on it, together with notice of the proceedings on form C6A. It should be served at least 14 days before the hearing, PD 12C accompanying the FPR 2010.

Under rule 12.3 of the FPR 2010, anyone may apply on form C2 to be joined as a respondent or may be made a respondent by court order without application. The same applies if respondents wish to be removed. If the person requesting party status has parental responsibility for the child, the court must grant that person's request.

13.8.5 Service

The rules about serving a document are contained in rules 6.23–6.39 of the FPR 2010 and the accompanying PD 6A. Service can be carried out by delivery to the solicitor acting for the person to be served, personally, by document exchange, facsimile transmission, email or by first class post; or by delivery to the person himself either personally or by first class post to his last known residence.

The court has the power under the rules to abridge, waive or vary the manner of service, rule 6.35 of the FPR 2010.

13.8.6 Applications made without notice (formerly known as *ex parte* procedures)

These are applications made without requiring the other party/parties to attend on notice. Applications for orders under section 8 of the CA 1989 may be made *without notice* in any court, rule 12.16 of the FPR 2010, but applicants will need leave of the justices clerk in the FPC, rule 12.16(3).

Applications made without notice must be supported by the same forms (form C100 or form C2) which should be brought to court or, if it is a telephone application, should be filed the next business day. In any event, they should be served on the respondents within 48 hours of any order being made. The court has the power under the rules to give directions as to service.

In the context of Article 6 of the European Convention for the Protection of Human Rights and Fundamental Freedoms 1950 and the interests of natural justice, applications without notice are generally frowned upon by the courts. They should be reserved for situations of extreme urgency, such as medical or other emergencies or child abduction cases, rule 12.47 of the FPR 2010.

13.8.7 Withdrawal, variation, discharge and appeals

Leave of the court is necessary for withdrawal of applications under section 8 of the CA 1989 (rule 29.4 of the FPR 2010) on oral application where the parties are present or by written request, setting out the reasons for withdrawal, which must then be duly served. The court may permit withdrawal without a hearing if the parties and any other person such as the CAFCASS officer have had a chance to make representations and the court considers it appropriate.

Applications to vary or discharge an order under section 8 of the CA 1989 may be made by those entitled to seek the original order, see paras 13.1–43.2, and applications at para 13.8. The procedure is the same as the original application. Under section 91(14), the court may order that no further application be made for a specified period without leave.

Orders under section 8 of the CA 1989 are automatically discharged by the making of a care order or an adoption order, see section 91(2).

An appeal may be lodged with the High Court under section 94(1) of the CA 1989 against a decision of an FPC concerning a section 8 order. Appeals against decisions made in the county court and High Court follow the general rules and lie to the Court of Appeal.

13.9   Family assistance order

Section 16 of the CA 1989 creates the family assistance order, requiring a probation or local authority officer to be made available to 'advise, assist and befriend' any person named in the order, section 16(1). But note that the court can only make this order with the consent of every person named in the order save the child, section 16(3).

The person to be 'advised assisted or befriended' may be the child, his or her parent or guardian, or any person with whom the child is living or who has a contact order in respect of the child, section 16(2). It originally lasted for six months, but has recently been extended to a possible maximum of 12 months, or a shorter specified period, section 16(5) of the CA 1989.

The family assistance order may direct the person(s) named in the order to take whatever steps are necessary to enable the officer to be kept informed of their address, and to be allowed to visit the named person, section 16(4) of the CA 1989.

Where there is in force a family assistance order and also an order under section 8 of the CA 1989, then the officer may refer to the court the possibility of variation or discharge of the section 8 order, section 16(6). This power should obviously be of use where a family assistance order has been made at the same time as a contact order which is clearly not working. Under section 16(4A) the officer concerned may specifically also assist in facilitating a contact order, if any.

13.10 Order to local authority to investigate under section 37 of the Children Act 1989

Where, in any 'family proceedings', see section 8(3) of the CA 1989, in which a question arises with respect to the welfare of any child, it appears to the court that it may be appropriate for a care or supervision order to be made, the court may direct the appropriate authority to undertake an investigation of the child's circumstances, section 37(1).

The local authority to whom the direction is given is then under a duty to consider whether it should:

* apply for a care or supervision order;

* provide services or assistance for the child and family;

* take any other action in respect of the child.

If the local authority decides not to seek a care order, it shall inform the court within eight weeks from the direction under section 37 of the CA 1989 of its reasons, any services or assistance provided, and any other action taken. If the decision is made to seek care or supervision, the local authority shall also consider whether it would be appropriate to review the case at a later date, and the date of any such review shall be determined.

A direction under section 37 of the CA 1989 is different to a section 7 direction, because the latter is not made because the court has concerns that care proceedings may be necessary, but because the family is already known by officers in the local authority.

13.11 Special guardianship

Note that special guardianship orders (see Chapter 3) are private law orders, coming within Part II of the CA 1989, sections 14A–F, and may be appropriately considered in some cases as an alternative to a residence order.

14 Commencement and Transfer of Proceedings

14.1 General rules

Under section 1 of the Family Law Act 1986, a child in respect of whom an application is made must be either ordinarily or habitually resident in England and Wales, or physically present within the jurisdiction of the court at the time of the application. The 1986 Act applies to applications under sections 8 and 14A–F (special guardianship) of the Children Act 1989 (CA 1989) and under the inherent jurisdiction of the High Court, but has been extended to care proceedings by case law.

The general rule is that private law applications under the CA 1989 may be made at any level of the court, but since the introduction of the Allocation and Transfer of Proceedings Order 2008, SI 2008/28, applications made to a county court are likely to be allocated to the family proceedings courts (FPCs) unless there are obvious issues of complexity. Some courts are now organised into family hearing centres, where a legal adviser will allocate the application to the appropriate level of court, county or FPC (see Figure 7).

Under paragraph 5(2) of the Allocation and Transfer of Proceedings Order 2008, the following types of application must be made to the FPC:

(a) section 4 of the CA 1989 (acquisition of parental responsibility by father);

(b) section 4A (acquisition of parental responsibility by step-parent)

In public law cases, the general rule is that proceedings should be commenced in the FPC, with specified exceptions, see para 14.2.

The county courts are divided into categories, each having the power to hear specified types of case. These are care centres, family hearing centres, adoption centres, inter-county adoption centres and forced marriage county courts. They are listed geographically in Schedule 1 to the Allocation and Transfer of Proceedings Order 2008. Applications under the Adoption and Children Act 2002 must be made to an adoption centre.

Figure 7 Commencement of proceedings

Children Act 1989 Section	Order	Applicant	Needs leave	Form	Court can make order of own volition	Family Proceedings Court	County Court	High Court
4	Parental responsibility	1. Child's father 2. Spouse or civil partner of parent with PR 3. second female parent of child		C1 together with FM1		Allocation and Transfer of Proceedings Order 2008 Articles 5(2) and 5(4)		
4(3)	Termination of PR	Person with PR Child, with leave of the Court	✓	C1 FM1		Allocation and Transfer of Proceedings Order 2008 Articles 5(2) and 5(4)		Termination of Proceedings Order 2008
5	Appoint Guardian	Anyone		C1 FM1	✓	Applicant's choice, subject to public funding restrictions Allocation and Transfer of Proceedings Order 2008 Article 9		
6	Terminate appt of Guardian	Anyone with PR Child, with leave of the Court	✓	C1 FM1		Applicant's choice, subject to public funding restrictions Allocation and Transfer of Proceedings Order 2008 Article 9		
8	Contact	Parent Guardian Person with Residence Order Party to marriage Person with care of child for 3 years or consent of those with PR	Anyone with leave may apply	C100 FM1 Possibly C1A	✓	Applicant's choice, subject to public funding restrictions Allocation and Transfer of Proceedings Order 2008 Article 9	Applicant's choice, subject to public funding restrictions Allocation and Transfer of Proceedings Order 2008 Article 9	Child's application for leave Also can transfer to High Court Articles 14-19 Allocation and Transfer of Proceedings Order 2008
8	Residence	Parent Guardian Person with Residence Order Party to marriage Person with care of child for 3 years or consent of those with PR Also, a relative with whom child has lived for previous 12 months – s36-38 CYPA 2008	Anyone with leave may apply	C100 FM1 Possibly C1A	✓	Applicant's choice, subject to public funding restrictions Allocation and Transfer of Proceedings Order 2008 Article 9		Child's application for leave Also can transfer to High Court Articles 14-19 Allocation and Transfer of Proceedings Order 2008
8	Prohibited Steps	Parent Guardian Person with Residence Order	* Anyone with leave may apply	C100 FM1 Possibly C1A	✓	Applicant's choice, subject to public funding restrictions Allocation and Transfer of Proceedings Order 2008 Article 9		Child's application for leave HIV tests Restriction of publicity International dimension Also can transfer to High Court Articles 14-19 Allocation and Transfer of Proceedings Order 2008

Children Act 1989 Section	Order	Applicant	Needs leave	Form	Court can make order of own volition	Family Proceedings Court	County Court	High Court
						Applicant's choice, subject to legal aid restrictions	Any court	
8	Specific Issue	Parent, Guardian, Person with Residence Order	* Anyone with leave may apply	C1 or C2	✓			Child seeks leave & able child disabled, blood products use, HIV tests, Restriction of publicity, International dimension
16	Family Assistance Order	Can only be made on the courts' volition with consent of the parties			✓			
25	Secure Accommodation	Local Authority, Area Health Auth., NHS Trust, Person caring in a residential home		C1 + Supplement C20		✓E	E = EXCEPTIONS: * Court directed investigations * Pending proceedings	
31	Care Order or Supervision Order	Local Authority or NSPCC		C1, C2 + Suppl. C13		✓E	* Extension variation or discharge of existing order	
34	Care Contact Order	Local Authority, Child, Anyone with leave		C1 or C2	Court can make s 34 order along with Care Order	✓E	May be commenced in the court in which direction given, proceedings are pending, or original order was made	
36	Education Supervision Order	Local Education Authority		Form C17 or C17A		✓E		
43	Child Assessment Order	Local Authority or NSPCC		C1 + Suppl C16		✓E		
44	Emergency Protection	Any Person		C1 with Suppl C11		✓E		
50	Recovery Order	Person with PR by care order or Emergency Protection order, Designated Officer		C1 with Suppl C18		✓E		

14.2 Specified exceptions to the general rules

Under the Allocation and Transfer of Proceedings Order 2008 applications for parental responsibility under sections 4 and 4A of the CA 1989 and public law proceedings may be commenced in the county court or the High Court if:

(a)   there are proceedings pending in that court; or

(b)   the application is for extension, variation or discharge of an existing order made by that court.

In these circumstances the application may be made to the court in which the proceedings are pending, or the existing order was made.

Applications made by children aged under 18 must normally be made to the county court.

14.2.1 Proceedings which must be commenced in the High Court

Under paragraph 7 of the Allocation and Transfer of Proceedings Order 2008, applications may be made to the High Court where:

(a)   the proceedings are exceptionally complex;

(b)   the outcome of the proceedings is important to the public in general; or

(c)   there is another substantial reason for the proceedings to be started in the High Court.

Case law suggests that certain proceedings should be heard at High Court level:

(a)   applications for authorisation of the use of blood products (e.g. where there is religious objection);

(b)   issues regarding life saving or life prolonging surgical intervention;

(c)   applications for post-adoption contact;

(d)   leave to submit a child to HIV tests;

(e)   contested issues concerning sterilisation or terminations of pregnancy of minors or mentally ill adults;

(f)   cases concerning international issues;

(g)   matters concerning restriction of general publicity;

(h)   applying for leave to withhold certain information from parties

However, the High Court must transfer to a county court or a magistrates' court any proceedings which were started in, or transferred to, the High Court in cases where the High Court considers that none of the criteria in paragraph 18 of the Allocation and Transfer of Proceedings Order 2008 (see para 14.2) applies. The High Court also has the power to refer some cases back to a county court, with consent of the parties or after hearing parties' representations.

14.3   Transfers

Transfers are also governed generally by the Allocation and Transfer of Proceedings Order 2008.

When proceedings are commenced in one level of the court, they may be transferred up or down the tiers if necessary, subject to the restrictions on venue outlined above. When transferring a case, the court must have regard to the principles in section 1 of the CA 1989, and in particular the avoidance of delay.

14.3.1   Transfers from family proceedings court to county court

Under paragraph 15(1) of the Allocation and Transfer of Proceedings Order 2008 a magistrates' court may transfer the whole or any part of proceedings to a county court only if the magistrates' court considers that:

(a)   the transfer will significantly accelerate the determination of the proceedings;

(b)   there is a real possibility of difficulty in resolving conflicts in the evidence of witnesses;

(c)   there is a real possibility of a conflict in the evidence of two or more experts;

(d)   there is a novel or difficult point of law;

(e)   there are proceedings concerning the child in another jurisdiction or there are international law issues;

(f) there is a real possibility that enforcement proceedings may be necessary and the method of enforcement or the likely penalty is beyond the powers of a magistrates' court;

(g) there is a real possibility that a guardian ad litem will be appointed under rule 16.4 of the Family Procedure Rules 2010, SI 2010/2955 (FPR 2010);

(h) there is a real possibility that a party to proceedings is a person lacking capacity within the meaning of the Mental Capacity Act 2005 to conduct the proceedings; or

(i) there is another good reason for the proceedings to be transferred.

Emergency protection orders and cases under section 25 of the CA 1989 (secure accommodation) may not be transferred up to a county court.

14.4 Transfer to High Court

Under paragraph 18 of the Allocation and Transfer of Proceedings Order 2008, a county court may transfer proceedings to the High Court only if the county court considers that:

(a) the proceedings are exceptionally complex;

(b) the outcome of the proceedings is important to the public in general; or

(c) there is another substantial reason for the proceedings to be transferred.

14.5 Transfer between courts

Proceedings may be transferred to another court at the same level if this would be more convenient for the parties or child, would accelerate proceedings, or for other good reason, paragraphs 14 and 17 of the Allocation and Transfer of Proceedings Order 2008.

14.6 Urgent applications

Subject to rules, guidance and case law on jurisdiction and venue (see paras 14.1–14.3), the referral procedures for urgent applications to the High Court are set out in PD 12E accompanying the FPR 2010.

Urgent applications should whenever possible be made within court hours. The earliest possible liaison is required with the Clerk who will attempt to accommodate genuinely urgent applications (at least for initial directions) in the Family Division applications court, from which the matter may be referred to another judge. When it is not possible to apply within court hours, contact should be made with the security office at the Royal Courts of Justice (see the HM Courts & Tribunals Service website for the relevant telephone numbers, www.justice.gov.uk/about/hmcts) who will refer the matter to the urgent business officer, who can contact the duty judge. The judge may agree to hold a hearing, either convened at court or elsewhere, or by telephone.

PD 12E accompanying the FPR 2010 includes guidance on liaising with Children and Family Court Advisory and Support Service (CAFCASS), CAFCASS Cymru or the Official Solicitor in urgent applications.

In mid-2012, the opening hours for court counter services in all civil courts were reduced to two hours on weekdays, being replaced by 'dropbox' facilities. Information on arrangements for urgent applications to county and magistrates' courts is available on a local basis.

15 Working with Children

15.1 Appointment and role of the children's guardian

The children's guardian is a person appointed by the court to act for a child aged under 18 years. In cases under the Children Act 1989 (CA 1989), a children's guardian should be appointed in 'specified family proceedings' (see section 41(6) and para 15.1.1) unless the court is satisfied that it is not necessary to do so, and may also be appointed in certain non-specified proceedings. The provisions governing the appointment and functioning of a children's guardian are in sections 41–42, and Parts 12, 14 and 16 of the Family Procedure Rules 2010, SI 2010/2955 (FPR 2010). In *A County Council v K and others* [2011] EWHC 1672 (Fam), the President of the Family Division clearly explains that the personal appointment of the guardian makes him or her accountable to the court for his or her professional judgment in representing the child's interests during proceedings.

The children's guardian should be independent and has a duty to investigate the circumstances of the case thoroughly, interviewing parties and witnesses and examining all available evidence. The children's guardian should interview all those who may be able to give relevant information about the child's life and circumstances and also the child and her family, and may request any necessary further information or assessments and then evaluate all the evidence. The children's guardian has a duty to advise the court of the child's wishes and feelings; to inform the court of the child's circumstances, bearing in mind the welfare checklist; to evaluate all the options open to the court; and lastly to advise the court on the best way forward in the interests of the child.

Children's guardians may be employees of the Children and Family Court Advisory and Support Service (CAFCASS) or they may be independent social workers who have a contractual arrangement with CAFCASS for the taking of cases (but not employed by) CAFCASS. See Chapter 4, para 4.6 for information about CAFCASS, which now comprises the former Children's Guardian and Reporting Officer Service, the Family Court Welfare Service and the Children's Branch of the Official Solicitor's Department, see sections 41–42 of the CA 1989, and Parts 12, 14 and 16 of the FPR 2010. In Wales, these functions are undertaken by CAFCASS Cymru, which operates under the Welsh Government.

Further information can be obtained from the CAFCASS website, www.cafcass.gov.uk, the CAFCASS Cymru website, http://wales.gov.uk/cafcasscymru and the website of NAGALRO (Professional Association for Children's Guardians, Family Court Advisers and Independent Social Workers), www.nagalro.com.

15.1.1   Official Solicitor

The Official Solicitor is an independent statutory office holder. His office (together with that of the Public Trustee) (OSPT) is an arm's length body of the Ministry of Justice. The Official Solicitor also acts as next friend or guardian ad litem of a child party whose own welfare is not the subject of family proceedings. The most common examples are listed in the *Practice Note, Official Solicitor: Appointment in Family Proceedings*, 2 April 2001. The Official Solicitor will seek to determine the child's best interests within the litigation and take all measures necessary within the proceedings for the child's benefit. Further information can be obtained from the Official Solicitor's Family Litigation Divisional Managers, telephone 020 7911 7132/7084 and from www.justice.gov.uk.

15.1.2   Public finding, access to information and disclosures

A child who is subject to 'specified proceedings' is entitled to publicly funded legal representation. A solicitor may be appointed for the child by the children's guardian or by the court. In the event of a conflict between the child and the children's guardian, a child of sufficient understanding may wish to choose his or her own solicitor, which is acceptable, provided that the appointment complies with section 41(3) of the CA 1989 and the duties of the solicitor under rule 16.29 of the FPR 2010.

The children's guardian has access under section 42(1) of the CA 1989 to all social work files and records and, if any of these documents are copied by the children's guardian, they are admissible in evidence before the court, section 42(2). See the case of *Re T* [1994] 1 FLR 632 in which the local authority refused to disclose records of potential adopters to the children's guardian, but the Court of Appeal ordered that the children's guardian should have access to them under the terms of section 42.

The children's guardian may ask for access to medical or psychiatric records of the child, and may wish to see the health records of others involved in the child's life. Note the leading case of *Oxfordshire CC v P* [1995] 1 FLR 582 concerning the issue of how confidential information should be treated by children's guardians.

The report of the children's guardian is confidential to the court and the parties, and permission of the court is required to disclose the report to others (or for use in other cases) and also to withhold information from parties. Leave to withhold information from parties may be sufficiently serious to warrant a High Court hearing, *Re M (Disclosure)* [1998] 2 FLR 1028. The power of the court to control evidence is set out in rule 22.1 of the FLR 2010.

The children's guardian in specified proceedings may bring applications on behalf of the child, or the child's solicitor, if the child is of sufficient age to instruct separately (see para 15.2).

See also *The Children Act 1989 Guidance and Regulations* (DCSF), Volume 7 *Guardians ad Litem and Other Court Related Issues*; *The SFLA Guide to Good Practice for Solicitors Acting for Children* (SFLA, 6th edn, 2002); *Representation of Children in Public Law Proceedings* (Law Society, 2006); and *Appointing a Solicitor for the Child in Specified Proceedings: Guidelines for the Courts* (Law Society, 2007).

15.1.3   Specified proceedings

Specified proceedings are defined in section 41(6) of the CA 1989.

Specified proceedings include applications for parental orders under section 30 of the Human Fertilisation and Embryology Act 1990.

15.2   Conflict between children's guardian and child

The child, if of sufficient age and understanding, may request client confidentiality with their solicitor, and/or disagree with the recommendations of the children's guardian.

In this case, the child's solicitor must decide: (a) whether the child is of sufficient age and understanding to instruct separately; and (b) whether there is a conflict between the child and the children's guardian. If both factors are present, the solicitor should discuss the matter with the children's guardian. Under rule 16.6 of the FPR 2010, a child may conduct proceedings without a children's guardian or litigation friend in specified circumstances. If a child radically disagrees with his or her children's guardian and is competent to instruct his or her own solicitor, then the court must be informed, and the solicitor may continue to represent the child client. The children's guardian will then proceed unrepresented or seek another lawyer where necessary.

The child of sufficient age may ask his or her solicitor to keep matters confidential, and disclosure is then an issue for the solicitor to decide. The Law Society (*Representation of Children in Public Law Proceedings* (Law Society, 2006)) allows a solicitor to breach the confidentiality of an immature child client where there is a risk of serious harm to the child or to others, but the guidance suggests that a mature ('*Gillick* competent') child may be entitled to confidentiality unless other children are at risk, or the child is in fear of his or her life or serious injury.

Another possible way to avoid ethical dilemmas for solicitors representing children (or adults in family matters) is to discuss confidentiality at the outset of taking instructions, and gain the client's agreement that, if a concern arises of a risk of serious harm to the client or to others, the solicitor has permission to disclose those concerns to the children's guardian or to an appropriate helping agency. This type of agreement is often used by other professionals, for example in mental health and medical care. Clients are usually willing to give their consent, and this avoids any subsequent ethical difficulty. Clients, especially young people and children, usually tell people that they trust about their problems because they would really like to have help. If the client wishes to keep the issues secret, his or her reasons for this should be discussed. Is the client afraid of reprisals or is he or she possibly protecting someone else? Is there anyone else the client feels he or she could trust with this information? Once the client's fear is known, appropriate resources can be looked for and the possibility of referrals which might be acceptable to the client can be explored. Clients often worry that the helping agencies, once told about the issues of concern, might let them down by failing to provide the help needed, leaving them or others exposed to continued risk. We can do something about that by agreeing to remain alongside the client and doing our best to ensure that they do receive effective and appropriate help, in the ways that they feel are right for them.

15.3 Should I see my child client?

When training solicitors for the Children Panel, we have been surprised by the number of solicitors who ask this question. In our view, lawyers representing children should, as a matter of good practice, meet with their child clients, unless, exceptionally, there is a cogent reason not to do so. However, the timing of the meeting is important and should be planned carefully, and the necessary arrangements should be made in co-operation with the children's guardian, the child's parents and carers, and the local authority, see paras 15.3.1 and 15.4.1.

We agree with Christine Liddle, who says in *Acting for Children* (Law Society, 1992), 'Although children vary in their ability to give instructions, it is still very beneficial to the solicitor's understanding of the case for him to meet his child client, whatever the age' (pp 5–6).

If a solicitor is to represent a child properly in court, it is necessary to understand the child's personality, behaviour, background and needs. This can be done through information gained by others, but it is best done at first hand. Even a small baby can non-verbally tell the observer a good deal about herself. Seeing a child client and interacting with him in his usual environment gives not only greater understanding of the child but also creates a sense of involvement with the client which encourages the solicitor to perceive the child as a person, rather than as an 'object of concern' or 'a case', *Acting for Children* (Law Society, 1992).

Public funding in public law proceedings is granted to the child client, through the children's guardian. Initially, the solicitor is instructed through the children's guardian and the court, but the solicitor should speak with child clients who appear to be of sufficient maturity, as a vital part of the preparation of the case, see Parts 12, 14 and 16 of the FPR 2010. The solicitor's task is to discover, firstly, whether the child is sufficiently mature to instruct a lawyer separately if necessary and, secondly, to find out whether a conflict exists between the child and the children's guardian. The solicitor also needs to elicit the child's wishes and feelings in order to represent them accurately to the court.

In addition to the guidance listed in para 15.1, in 2006, the Law Society, with Resolution, the Legal Services Commission and the Department for Constitutional Affairs produced the 2nd edition of *The Family Law Protocol* (available at www.lawsociety.org.uk) applicable in private law proceedings. For solicitors involved in public law proceedings, see *The Good Practice Guide in Child Care Cases* (The Law Society, 2010).

15.3.1 Meeting a child client

When arranging to meet a child, consideration should be given to the most appropriate setting and style for such a meeting. Interviews should be short and at the child's pace.

Pat Monro and Lis Forrester in *The Children's Guardian* (Family Law, 1995) assume that solicitors will meet their child clients, adding practical advice:

> Where a young child is involved, the instructions will come from the children's guardian and it will usually be appropriate for the children's guardian to meet with the child in the first instance without the solicitor, who can be introduced at a later date. A young child will probably be confused by the introduction of a number of new faces, and therefore it is important for the children's guardian to get to know the child before the solicitor becomes involved. (p 46)

Note: There are rare cases where it may be inappropriate for the solicitor to meet with his or her child client, for example where the child is severely emotionally damaged and the introduction of a new person may adversely affect the child. For further notes, see para 15.4.1.

15.3.2 Decisions concerning a child's competence

The Good Practice Guide in Child Care Cases (The Law Society, 2010) comments that a solicitor's professional training is not well designed to equip him or her to make an assessment of a child's understanding unaided, although solicitors, particularly those on the Children Panel, will have a certain amount of knowledge through experience and/or will have undergone some level of training in the basics of child development.

Clearly, the expectation is that solicitors will discuss the issue of their child client's competence with the experts in both public law and private cases. The children's guardian in a public law case is the first person to be consulted on the issue. Child psychologists, psychiatrists, counsellors and others working with the child will also have useful views.

The rights of the child are set out in Chapter 12, including the competence of a child to instruct a solicitor or to give consent to assessments and treatments depending on the child's mental capacity, maturity and level of understanding of the situation. See Chapter 12 for further discussion of the concept of *'Gillick* competence', which evolved from the case of *Gillick v West Norfolk and Wisbech AHA* [1986] AC 112. Chapter 3 addresses parental responsibility. Please note that those who hold parental responsibility for a child will make decisions for those children who do not have competence.

15.4 Taking instructions and communicating with children

Good communication with children is essential if instructions are to be effective. A basic understanding of child development, confidence in being with children (preferably accrued through practical experience) and integrity are vital. Children tend to ask direct questions, they dislike being patronised and will quickly see through prevarication. They deserve the respect of straight answers to any questions they ask, given in age-appropriate language.

Older children clients may like to receive an age-appropriate letter to let them know that they have a solicitor and to provide a channel of communication which they can take up themselves if they are worried or curious or simply want to communicate about anything. Solicitors may communicate by telephone, text or email with older children. A few stamped envelopes (addressed to the solicitor's office) plus a mobile telephone number and an email address sent with the introductory letter enable the child to phone, text or write back if she wishes. It also empowers her – she has the information and the means to communicate and respond – so she will not be reliant on others to get in touch with her solicitor, and she can personally get in touch confidentially and quickly if necessary.

Younger children may like to give or send their solicitor notes or drawings, etc. and may like to receive a proper reply (cards are good for this). Getting an age-appropriate, suitable card from your own solicitor is a great boost for confidence. Space may be needed on the office walls for the many drawings that will inevitably accumulate.

Everyone has their own way of communicating with others, so there are no hard and fast rules. A few guidelines which may be of use are set out below.

15.4.1 Guidelines on effective meetings and communication with children

- Discuss the timing of the first meeting with the carers for the child, the child himself and with the children's guardian.

- Consult the children's guardian about whether to accompany the guardian on his or her first visit to the child.

- Find out what the children's guardian has already told the child about the case. Ask what has been said to the child about the role of children's guardian and solicitor and how much of the facts it is appropriate to tell the child or to discuss with her.

- Explain clearly and honestly issues of confidentiality to the child, in age-appropriate language.

- Children do not like being patronised. Answer questions as directly and openly as is appropriate, and explain and discuss issues with children in age-appropriate language.

- Informal clothing is best, not formal or intimidating 'power dressing' clothes, but look professional.

- Position yourself on the same level as young clients, it is acceptable to sit on the floor to talk/play.

- Take a few props to help communication if you are comfortable with using them, such as: paper, crayons or pencils (not felt tips, sharp pens, messy biros or your best fountain pen), creative bendy sticks, glove puppets, small toys, a doll family, toy transport, for example bus/car/van/bike, toy mobile or phone, etc.

- Do not worry if you do not feel at ease playing with toys. It is also totally acceptable to just *talk* with children, and even more important to listen.

- Do not take sweets, food, messy pens, biros or felt tipped pens (these can upset carers, tummies, or ruin furniture).

- Ask the child what he or she wishes to be called. Names are important. Does the child have preferred names for herself or others?

- Try to understand the child and the environment in which he or she has been living. Get the child to talk about favourite/least favourite television programmes, activities, pop stars, food, colours, clothes, football teams, toys, friends, music, games, people and pets.

- Usually, the guardian will have introduced the solicitor to the child, but if not, then, once the child is at ease, explain your role as his or her solicitor. Many older children have seen lawyers on television and have varying ideas about the legal system, ranging from the totally Dickensian lawyer to the American advocate, or they may have ideas based on scenes from current films and TV crime series. The explanation needs to be age appropriate. It could be something along these lines:

I am your solicitor. Part of my job is to go along to the court and talk to the court/judge/magistrates and to tell them how you feel about what is happening now, and what you would like to happen.

I would like to talk with you and I want to understand. I promise to listen, because I want to hear what you would like to tell me.

Most children feel at some level that they are not listened to, and a promise to listen carefully and really pay attention to what they say is important. There will be much more to explain and discuss with a child client, but this is a good start.

- Explain to the child what the proceedings are about, in an age-appropriate way.

- There are books to help explain who is who in court, etc. (see Chapter 19).

- End the meeting when the child indicates he or she has had enough. Concentrating may be difficult for any length of time for a child, especially in a stressful situation. Do not overtire a young child, or overstay: an hour or less is usually enough.

- Do not try to press a child for facts, especially about past traumatic events, as it may cause emotional distress, which the child's carers then have to deal with afterwards.

- Avoid questioning a child intrusively. Involve the child's carers if help is needed to engage the child, and end the visit if the child seems unwilling to continue.

- Never distress a child by being 'pushy' if he or she does not want to talk or by overstaying. The children's guardian will assist with advice or help, or if the solicitor is unsure, a joint visit to the child can be made.

- A sense of calm, goodwill and appropriate humour usually help.

15.5   Child development

There is insufficient space in this book to discuss child development in any detail. There are a number of excellent reference books on the market, some of which are listed here, and see also Chapter 19.

The contribution by Mary Sheridan in *Assessing children in need and their families: Practice Guidance* (DoH, 2000), Appendix 1, contains concise, useful information on child development from birth to five years.

Another useful book used by lawyers and children's guardians is KS Holt, *Child Development – Diagnosis and Assessment* (Butterworths, 1994).

HB Valman, *ABC of One to Seven* (British Medical Association, 4th edn, 1999) is useful, and many bookshops carry a range of books on child development intended for parents which practitioners will find readable and helpful.

15.6   Understanding your child client – race, religion, culture and ethnicity

The welfare checklist pays attention to the child's 'physical educational and emotional needs', section 1(3)(b) of the CA 1989; and 'age, sex, background and any characteristics of his which the court considers relevant', section 1(3)(d).

Although the CA 1989 does not refer specifically to race, religion and culture, they are clearly included in these categories. If the child's background and needs arising from it are not clear to the solicitor and children's guardian, then expert assistance should be sought from someone who fully understands the child's cultural, religious and social needs. The child may also have physical needs which may have to be explained to a carer from a different culture, for example, food, religious taboos and customs, hair and skin care, etc. Quite often, behaviour which would not make sense within one culture in a given situation makes perfect sense when understood in the context of another. The court must take the child's needs fully into account when deciding the most appropriate way forward to promote and safeguard the child's welfare.

15.7   After the case is over

Children often develop a relationship of trust with their solicitor, and, whatever the outcome of the case, may want to keep in touch. The children's guardian's role ceases for that child when the final order is made. By contrast, the solicitor is a continuing source of help and a useful contact in the outside world. Children may be pleased to have their own solicitor who they can contact or ask about problems as they arise, particularly as they reach their teenage years.

It is good to have a final visit to a child client and to let him or her have a business card to keep if he or she is old enough to use it. A few sheets of blank paper, and stamped addressed envelopes can be left in case the child wants to write. The child may want to phone, text, email or call into the office. If a child makes contact, make a point of responding immediately, and in a way appropriate for the child's age and understanding.

Children who are in care need to know their rights, and these should have been explained by children's services. If a child is concerned about the standard of care he or she is receiving, or has a need to complain, the solicitor may be the first person the child thinks of to talk to about the problem. Older children may at some time wish to instruct a solicitor on their own behalf to apply for an order under section 8 of the CA 1989, or to apply to discharge a care order, so it is essential to keep an avenue of communication open for them.

Often, the child may be concerned about an aspect of his or her care, and the solicitor can perform a useful function in explaining and mediating between the child and parents or child and officers or agencies when difficulties arise.

When leaving care, older children also have the right to additional services under the Children (Leaving Care) Act 2000, and they may wish to seek advice about the ways in which their needs can be met.

Case records, statements and documents should be kept at least until the child reaches 21. In adoption cases, records may need to be kept longer. Guardians working from home are required to return their case papers to CAFCASS for archiving and are not permitted to retain any information at all in relation to the case, including copies of reports that they have written. Thus if there are future applications it may be rather crucial that the child's solicitor has retained a full set of papers, particularly if the previous guardian is not available or if the archiving system is unable to quickly locate old papers.

It goes without saying that cases are confidential and need to be kept (and eventually destroyed) securely.

15.8 Judges seeing children in private law proceedings

Judges should be very careful about when and how they see children in the course of private law proceedings.

In the recent case of *Re W* [2008] EWCA Civ 538, [2008] All ER (D) 258 (May), the Court of Appeal gave useful guidance on this in relation to a judge seeing a child of 15 years of age:

• the decision to see a child or not is in the discretion of the court;

• that discretion should be used cautiously;

- the recommended time and place is in chambers after submissions;

- the child should be seen at court;

- the judge should not promise confidentiality;

- the judge should summarise the salient points of the interview for the parties.

A reading of the full judgment in this case is recommended, along with *Representation of Children in Public Law Proceedings* (Law Society, 2006), mentioned in this chapter.

16 Assessment of Children in Need and Care Planning

16.1 New developments and materials

Following the Quality Protects Programme, to 'ensure that referral and assessment processes discriminate effectively between different types and level of need, and produce a timely response' (John Hutton, Minister of State for Social Services, March 2000), it seems that there is still considerable progress yet to be made. To facilitate the implementation of the Quality Protects Programme, the Department of Health set up steering and advisory groups, and the Department of Health, the Departments for Education and Employment and the Home Office issued new materials to provide guidance, practice material, and training resources. The emphasis is on evidence-based practice, and careful consideration of the needs of the individual child, with an expectation that inter-agency child protection and social work practice is based on analysis, reflection, and sound judgment in decision making.

Two major assessment materials are the companion volumes, *Framework for the assessment of children in need and their families* (DoH, 2000) and *Assessing children in need and their families: Practice Guidance* (DoH, 2000). Both of these are essential reference material for child protection practice. They replace the old 'Orange Book', *Protecting Children: A Guide to Social Workers Undertaking a Comprehensive Assessment* (DoH, 1988), but they still refer to Mary Sheridan's very useful basic child development charts for children from birth to five years.

Additional resources are *Initial and Core Assessment Records* (DoH, 2000) for children of different age groups and *Family Assessment Pack of Questionnaires and Scales* (DoH, 2000).

Note that the new *Working Together to Safeguard Children, A guide to inter-agency working to safeguard and promote the welfare of children* (DCSF, 2010) replaces all earlier versions. There may be a revised (shorter) version produced soon, so watch for developments.

The *Family Assessment Pack of Questionnaires and Scales* is a contribution to the assessment process by Cox and Bentovim, providing a set of measurement scales for different family situations including questionnaires on:

- strengths and difficulties (screening for emotional and behavioural problems);

- parenting daily hassles (screening for parenting stressors);

- adult well-being (screening for irritability, depression and anxiety);

- home conditions (family cleanliness, etc.);

- adolescent well-being (for self rating for depression);

- family activity (in different age bands 2–6 and 7–12 years) (child-centredness);

- recent life events (life events as potential stressors);

- alcohol scale (screening for alcohol overuse).

Other measuring instruments are now available: A Cox and S Walker, *The HOME Inventory – Home Observation and Measurement of the Environment* (Pavilion Publishing, 2002) and A Bentovim and L Bingley Miller, *The Family Assessment of Family Competence, Strengths and Difficulties* (Brighton Publishing, 2001).

16.1.2   Training materials

- *The Child's World, Assessing Children in Need, Training and Development Pack* (DoH, 2000) is put together by the NSPCC and the University of Sheffield. It contains a video, training guide, and a reader.

- J Howarth (ed.), *The Child's World: The Comprehensive Guide to Assessing Children in Need*, (Jessica Kingsley, 2nd edn, 2010).

- Children and Family Court Advisory and Support Service (CAFCASS) has introduced a plethora of 'tools' for working with both children and adults, available from the CAFCASS website, www.cafcass.gov.uk. These include the *My Needs, Wishes and Feelings Pack* and the *Domestic Violence Tool Kit* (Version 2.1, 2007), available at www.cafcass.gov.uk.

16.2   Assessment Framework

A child who is at risk of harm is by definition deemed to be 'a child in need'. Therefore all the guidance materials listed above apply to children who are subject to care proceedings, and also apply to many other children who may be assessed for the provision of resources by a local authority under section 17 of and Schedule 2 to the Children Act 1989 (CA 1989).

In *Assessing children in need and their families: Practice Guidance* (DoH, 2000), the assessment framework is depicted for clarity in the form of a triangle (see Figure 8). The child and the safeguarding and promoting of his welfare are central to the assessment process. Each limb of the triangle thus represents a particular area or domain of the child's world, which is further broken down into that domain's component parts, all of which inter-relate, and all of which need careful consideration both at an individual level and then as the whole picture.

The key areas are:

(a)   the first limb of the child's developmental needs broadly looks at the child's emotional, social and behavioural development and function, including a consideration of his identity; this limb also considers the child's physical health, his self-care skills and his educational development;

(b)   the second limb considers the parenting capacity of the child's carers and, as might be expected, includes an appraisal of the provision of basic care, nurture, stimulation, guidance and boundaries, stability and emotional warmth;

(c)   the third limb considers family and environmental factors, including the family history and functioning, the wider family, housing, employment, income, the family's social integration and the availability of community resources.

The structure of this assessment framework has been specifically designed to provide a systematic method for the gathering and analysing of information about children, in order that different types and levels of need can be more effectively identified.

Assessing children in need and their families looks also at the needs of children from other cultural and ethnic groups. It points out that this assessment model is equally applicable to disabled children and their families, however, the needs of the carers should be a particular factor to be taken into account.

The chapters each contain a significant body of reference material for further reading and research. The final chapter looks at resources to assist effective assessment, introducing the *Family Assessment Pack of Questionnaires and Scales* (DoH, 2000), and setting out the principles for use of the materials. The age-related set of *Initial and Core Assessment Records* (DoH, 2000) are an additional assessment tool.

See also *The Children Act Now: Messages from Research* (DoH, 1999) which summarises the major Department of Health commissioned studies on the CA 1989.

16.3   Care planning

Practitioners should note that case law precedent has already established the requirement for a care plan in applications under section 31 of the CA 1989. The emphasis now is on the nature, format and content of the care plan. See, also, Chapter 7, para 7.8.

More time is spent in the consideration of the care plan than almost any other aspect of care proceedings. It is far less likely that there will be a contest over the threshold criteria than a dispute over the proposed plan for the child.

No care order may be made unless the court has first considered a care plan submitted by the local authority, section 31(3A) of the CA 1989 and see LAC 99(29). The courts may require evidence in support of care plans and ask for placement details to be made available. Once the care order is made, the court loses control over implementation of the care plan. In *Re S (Minors) (Care Order: Implementation of Care Plan)*, *Re W (Minors) (Care Order: Adequacy of Care Plan)* [2002] UKHL 10, [2002] 1 FLR 815, the House of Lords affirmed the right of local authorities to discharge their responsibility under care orders without interference from the courts. However, since this case was heard, the role of the Independent Reporting Office was introduced to protect the interests of the child, section 118 of the Adoption and Children Act 2002, now in section 26 of the CA 1989.

If the grounds are satisfied, much of the court's time will then be spent on considering proportionality, and assessment and discussion of the timetable and care plan, in order to make the best decision for the child's short- and long-term future. However, the *Family Justice Review* (*Family Justice Review Final Report* (Ministry of Justice, 2011)) has identified this as a cause of unnecessary delay and has recommended that courts' scrutiny of care plans be curtailed.

LAC 99(29) sets out the contents of the care plan, in five sections:

(a)   overall aim;

(b)   child's needs including contact;

(c)   views of others;

(d)   placement details and timetable;

(e)   management and support by local authority.

Figure 8   Child assessment framework

Each child must have his or her own individual care plan, this also applies to sibling groups. The plan must be a separate document, and in the case of a final care plan should not only be signed by the social worker responsible for compiling the plan, but should also be endorsed by one or more 'relevant senior officers' from within the local authority.

The local authority should provide interim care plans in order that the court has the necessary information available before making interim orders. The circular indicates that during proceedings the numbering of care plans is desirable to reduce confusion, and to ensure that parties know which care plan is in operation.

The format of the care plan is set out in detail in LAC 99(29), paragraphs 15–18. There is commentary about care plans and assessment which relates to the new framework for the assessment of children in need (paragraph 23), the needs of disabled children (paragraph 26), race, culture, religion and language (paragraph 27) and care planning prior to adoption (paragraphs 28–33).

Copies of LAC (99)29 can still be obtained from the DoH website, www.dh.gov.uk. Other circulars can also be obtained from this website.

16.4   Adoption issues

The adoption law has been reformed, and a raft of new legislation has been developed. It is not within the ambit of this book to discuss adoption in detail, but adoption legislation, regulations and court rules are listed at www.education.gov.uk.

16.4.1   Legislation

For reference, please see the following, all of which can be read in full at www.legislation.gov.uk (statutes and statutory instruments) and www.education.gov.uk (other materials):

- Adoption and Children Act 2002.

- Adoption and Children (Scotland) Act 2007.

- Adopted Children and Adoption Contact Registers Regulations 2005, SI 2005/924.

- Adoption Agencies and Independent Review of Determinations (Amendment) Regulations 2011, SI 2011/589.

- Adoption Agencies (Panel and Consequential Amendments) Regulations 2012 (timetabled for commencement in September 2012), SI 2012/1410.

- Adoption Agencies Regulations 2005, SI 2005/389 (amended 2011).

- Adoption and Children (Miscellaneous Amendments) Regulations 2005, SI 2005/3482.

- Adoption Information and Intermediary Services Regulations 2005, SI 2005/890.

- Adoption Support Services Regulations 2005, SI 2005/691.

- Adoption Agencies (Wales) Regulations 2005, SI 2005/1313.

- Adoptions with a Foreign Element Regulations 2005, SI 2005/392.

- Adoption National Minimum Standards 2011.

- Adoption Statutory Guidance issued February 2011 (amended April 2011, see www.education.gov.uk).

- Disclosure of Adoption Information (Post-Commencement Adoptions) Regulations 2005, SI 2005/888.

- Family Procedure Rules 2010, SI 2010/2955.

- Independent Review of Determinations (Adoption and Fostering) Regulations 2009, SI 2009/395.

- Independent Review of Determinations (Adoption and Fostering) (Wales) Regulations 2010, SI 2010/746.

- Restriction on the Preparation of Adoption Reports Regulations 2005, SI 2005/1711.

- Suitability of Adopters Regulations 2005, SI 2005/1712.

16.4.2 Independent Review Mechanism

The Independent Review Mechanism (IRM) helps to build public confidence in the adoption service and the adopter assessment process. For those seeking more information on the IRM in relation to adoptions, see www.independentreviewmechanism.org.uk/panels.

16.4.3 Publications

There are a number of excellent publications listed in Chapter 19 which explain the new adoption law and practice. Further information about adoption law and practice issues can be obtained from the British Association for Adoption and Fostering and other adoption organisations listed in Chapter 19.

17 Appeals and Enforcement

17.1 Appeals and judicial review

Appeals are discussed briefly in this book under each topic, but since there is limited space, it is only possible to give further references for judicial review, complaints procedures and appeals procedures. D Hershman and A McFarlane (eds), *Children Law and Practice* (Family Law), Volume 1, section 1 has an excellent section on judicial review and appeals. Other useful books are J Manning, *Judicial Review Proceedings* (Family Law, 2004) and M Fordham, *Judicial Review Handbook* (Family Law, 2008).

17.1.1 Family proceedings court appeals to the county court

There is no 'slip rule', and no power to review or re-hear a decision. What is pronounced by the chair of the Bench must be written up as the order, and amendment can only happen if the words are not accurately written down. Since 6 April 2009, family proceedings court (FPC) orders under the Children Act 1989 (CA 1989) and the Adoption and Children Act 2002 are now challenged by notice of appeal to the county court within 21 days. This period is reduced to seven days if the appeal is against an interim care order under section 38 of the CA 1989.

Section 111A of the CA 1989, inserted into the Magistrates' Courts Act 1980 by the Access to Justice (Destination of Appeals) (Family Proceedings) Order 2009, SI 2009/871, provides that in family proceedings a person may appeal to a county court on the ground that a decision is wrong in law or is in excess of jurisdiction.

17.1.2 County court appeals

Appeal lies from decisions of the district judge to a judge of the same court, see PD 30A accompanying the Family Procedure Rules 2010, SI 2010/2955 (FPR 2010).

Notice must normally be filed within 21 days of the decision (rule 30.4(2) of the FPR 2010).

The county court has the power to review a decision and will allow an appeal where the decision was: (a) wrong; or (b) unjust because of serious procedural or other irregularity (rule 30.12(3) of the FPR 2010).

An appeal against a decision made by a circuit judge or recorder is to the Court of Appeal.

17.1.3 High Court appeals

Appeal lies from decisions of a district judge to a judge of the same court, for rehearing, no leave required, PD 30A accompanying the FPR 2010. The grounds are the same as above under rule 30.12(3).

17.1.4 Court of Appeal

Where the court from or to which an appeal is made considers that the appeal to be heard by the county or High Court raises an important point of principle or practice, or there is some other compelling reason for the Court of Appeal to hear it, the county court or High Court may order it to be transferred to the Court of Appeal (rule 30.13 of the FPR 2010).

17.2 Complaints procedures

If any person wishes to complain about any action by the children's services department in relation to a child, the procedure is set out in the Children Act 1989 Representations Procedure (England) Regulations 2006, SI 2006/1738 and the Representations Procedure (Children) (Wales) Regulations 2005, SI 2005/3365 (W. 262).

If a complainant is not satisfied by the local authority's response, he or she may be able to take the matter up with the Local Government Ombudsman (England) or the Public Services Ombudsman for Wales.

17.3 Enforcement

Enforcement of orders made under the CA 1989 is discussed briefly in this book under each topic. Further detail is available from D Hershman and A McFarlane (eds), *Children Law and Practice* (Family Law), Volume 1, which has an excellent section on enforcement of orders under the CA 1989 and a helpful table of enforcement procedures for orders under the CA 1989. See, also, Figure 9.

Figure 9   Enforcement procedures for orders under the Children Act

Breach of Order	Injunction/Penal Notice	Surety Bond	Committal or Contempt	Other remedy available	Police Powers and Criminal Proceedings
Refusal to give up a child for Residence Order			RSC Ord 45 r 7 CCR Ord 29 r 1 High Court or County Court may commit Family Proc Court may use s 63(3) MCA 1980	Search and Recovery Order s 34 Family Law Reform Act 1986 'Seek & Find' High Court Inherent jurisdiction	
Threat to remove child from UK, or actual removal attempt		can be used to ensure return of child	as above	1) Port Alert System 2) Passport Restriction	1) Police duty to assist where threat of danger or breach of the peace 2) Child Abduction & Custody Act 1985 offence
Change of name when child subject to residence order w/o consent or leave	✓		✓		
Refusal to comply with s 8 Contact Order	To use penal notice the acts to be enforced must be set out clearly in the order		Committal is rare, but possible	S 11(7) Directions, including contact activities; also s 111 CA 1989 warnings and enforcement	
Breach of specific issue or prohibited steps	✓		✓		Police duty to assist where threat of danger may be used in medical emergency
Removal of child from care (under s 31 order)	If removal from jurisdiction is threatened		✓	Port alert if threat to remove from UK High Court Tipstaff if threat to remove from jurisdiction Recovery order s 50 Children Act 1989	Child Abduction & Custody Act 1985 offence Police duty to assist where threat of danger may be used in medical emergency
Change of name of child in s 31 care without leave/consent	✓		✓		
Failure to produce records to guardian ad litem in care/supervision proceedings	Application to produce documents under s 42 Children Act 1989		Application to court to produce documents under s 42 Children Act 1989		
Breach of directions of the court in Children Act 1989 proceedings, as to filing, service or attendance				Wasted Costs Order • Court may impose adjournment, or proceed in absence of party • Evidence may be disallowed – but rare in Children Act cases	

18 Expert Evidence

18.1 What is an expert witness?

An 'expert witness' has no legal definition. Many professionals style themselves as 'expert witnesses', but it is the court which makes the final decision as to who is accepted as an expert in a particular specialist field, in each individual case. We have for example, seen a young, newly qualified nursery nurse treated by the court as an expert in the case of a particular child with whom she had worked intensively for a year. She would not have thought of claiming that status herself, but the court regarded her as an expert in that specific piece of work with that particular child. Other professionals might wish to claim expert status in their field of work, but the court may decide otherwise.

Experts are privileged in the eyes of the law – they are not restricted to evidence of fact and can give their opinion on any relevant matter in which they are appropriately qualified. Acceptance of a specialist as an expert, therefore, will vary according to the issues in each case, and in order to assess expertise, the court will expect that the expert will outline his or her qualifications and experience.

18.2 Choosing and instructing expert witnesses

The choice of the appropriate expert for a case is never an easy one, and the choice may be limited by availability and time frames. See para 18.4 for ideas derived from practice.

Part 25 of the FPR 2010 relates to experts and assessors, and under rule 25.1 the court has a duty to restrict expert evidence. The court may refuse permission to call an expert, but be aware that it may be argued that this may prejudice the right of the party to a fair trial under Article 6 of the European Convention for the Protection of Human Rights and Fundamental Freedoms 1950 (ECHR), see the case of *Elsholz v Germany* (2002) 34 EHRR 58, [2000] 2 FLR 486.

In the course of proceedings in the High Court, Wall J gave helpful guidance on the use of expert witnesses in his judgments, see *Re M (Minors) (Care Proceedings: Children's Wishes)* [1994] 1 FLR 749 and *Re G (Minors) (Expert Witnesses)* [1994] 2 FLR 291. See, also, The Rt Hon

Lord Justice Wall and I Hamilton, *A Handbook for Expert Witnesses in Children Act Cases* (Family Law, 2nd edn, 2007). Written for witnesses, but also good reading for lawyers, the book sets out in detail the way in which experts can expect to be approached, issues concerning disclosure, the preparation of instructions and reports.

18.2.1 Funding issues and prior authority from the Legal Services Commission to instruct expert witnesses

On 3 May 2012, Sir Nicholas Wall, President of the Family Division gave judgment in the case of *A Local Authority v DS, DI and DS* [2012] EWHC 1442 (Fam). The judgment was handed down in private and is signed by the President, with leave for it to be reported. In that judgment he gives guidance on the issue of prior authority from the Legal Services Commission (LSC) to instruct expert witnesses in publicly funded family proceedings.

The judgment is worth reading. Quotations include:

> For present purposes, the law can be taken quite shortly. To the mind of the lawyer it remains curious that an administrative body can effectively render nugatory a judicial decision taken in what the court perceives as the best interests of a child. Where the party or parties who seek to instruct an expert are publicly funded, however, there is no doubt that the LSC has the power, given to it by Parliament, to refuse to fund the instruction or to fund the instruction in part only. Moreover, the LSC undoubtedly has the power, deriving from the same source, to cap the level of fees which may be expended by the expert at a given level. That is undoubted the law. Lawyers may complain that this is an unfair state of affairs, or that they cannot find experts who will work at the rates laid down. Their remedy, if they take the view that the decision of the LSC is *Wednesbury* unreasonable or can be struck down for any other public law reason, is to apply for judicial review. ([2012] EWHC 1442 (Fam) at [38])

Guidance

45 In all the circumstances of this case, therefore, I feel able to offer the following general guidance:-

    i)   The words 'the cost thereof is deemed to be a necessary and proper disbursement on [a named individual's] public funding certificate' (or words to equivalent effect) should no longer be used when the court orders a report from an expert. The words do not bind the LSC or, for that matter anybody else. In addition, there must be doubt about the court's power to make such an order. It is, in my judgment, far better to follow the words of the

Regulations, particularly if the court is being asked to approve rates in excess of those allowed by the Funding Order. A copy of such an order is attached at the end of this judgment.

ii) The test for expert evidence will shortly import the word 'necessary'. The question which the court will have to ask itself is whether or not the report of the expert is necessary for the resolution of the case. FPR rule 25.1 will shortly be amended to insert the word 'necessary' for 'reasonably required' and there will be a new Practice Direction.

iii) It is the court which makes the order for the instruction of an expert, and this responsibility neither can nor should be delegated to the parties. It is of the essence of good case management that the court should identify the issues on which it wants the expert to report. It would thus be helpful and important for the tribunal to be able to say – if it is the case and the hard pressed Tribunal with a long list has had the time – that it has read all the (relevant) papers.

iv) If the court takes the view that an expert's report is *necessary* for the resolution of the case, it should say so, *and give its reasons.* This can be done by a preamble to the order, or by a short judgment, delivered at dictation speed or inserted by the parties with the judge's approval. I have considered this point carefully, and have come to the conclusion that this does not impose an undue burden either on the court or the profession.

v) There is no substitute for reasons. A consent order is still an order of the court: it is a judicial decision and must be supported by reasons. Equally, a decision by the LSC is a decision. It too should be supported by reasons.

vi) 'Reasons' in circumstances such as these need not be lengthy or elaborate. They must, however, explain to anyone reading them *why* the decision maker has reached the conclusion he or she has particularly if the expert is seeking to be paid at rates which are higher than those set out in the table in Schedule 6 of the Funding Order.

vii) Speed is of the essence in proceedings relating to children. An application for prior authority must be made at the earliest opportunity and, once again, must be carefully drafted and supported by reasons.

viii) By like token, it behoves the LSC to deal with such applications promptly and, particularly if the application is being refused, or only granted to a limited extent, to give its reasons for its decision. Once again, the reasons can be concise. Of course the solicitor seeking prior authority can go ahead regardless, and instruct the expert at the rates the expert demands, but such a suggestion, in reality, is unreal. The expert's contract is with the solicitor, and if he or she does not recover the expert's costs from the LSC, it is the solicitor who is liable. Given the exiguous rates of remuneration, this is a risk no solicitor is willing to take, particularly where the client is impecunious.

ix) Similar considerations to those set out above apply to any challenge to the LSC's ruling.

x) If a case is urgent, it should be so marked and the reasons for its urgency explained.

xi) Courts should familiarise themselves with Part 25 of the FPR and with Practice Direction 25A which supplements it. Specifically, they should be aware of paragraph 4.3(h) or its equivalent when amended which provides that the person wishing to instruct an expert must explain to the court why the expert evidence proposed cannot be given by Social Services undertaking a core assessment or by the Children's Guardian in accordance with their respective statutory duties. The Rule and the Practice Direction are being revised to make them (it is to be hoped) more practical and "user friendly". Practitioners should look out, in due course, for the amendments. ([2012] EWHC 1442 (Fam) at [45])

The President goes on to give general guidance, pointing out that the instruction of an expert should not delay a case, which should be conducted within the time frame of the Rules, the *Public Law Outline* (PLO) and the Practice Direction. He also gives a coda for the suggested form of order.

18.3   Expert witness evidence

If you are instructed to give evidence and unsure of procedure, P Pressdee et al, *The Public Law Outline: The Court Companion* (Family Law, 2008) provides an excellent comprehensive guide to the PLO.

See, also, PD 25A accompanying the FPR 2010.

The Civil Evidence Act 1972 applies to family proceedings in the High Court, county court and the family court, section 5. See also Part 25 of the FPR 2010 for rules relating to expert evidence in Children Act 1989 (CA 1989) cases, Order 38, rules 35–44 of the Rules of the Supreme Court 1965, SI 1965/1776, and Order 20, rules 27–28 of the County Court Rules 1981, SI 1981/1687.

18.3.1   Expert instruction checklist

Leave, consents and preliminary enquiries of experts

- When considering which expert to instruct, the court needs some information about the experts to decide which is appropriate.

- The experts may need some information about the case to decide whether to accept instructions. Provision of such anonymised information will not require prior consent, see PD 25A accompanying the FPR 2010. However, if experts need to check on the names of the parties for conflicts of interest before accepting instructions, consent to disclose the names would be required.

- Obtain all necessary leave for instruction of expert (see rule 12.74 of the FPR 2010) and for examination of a child before instructing the expert (see rule 12.20).

- Obtain leave of the court for disclosure of necessary documents to the expert before sending them to the expert (FPR 2010) (provision of information or documents in a case without authority may be contempt of court, see PD 25A accompanying the FPR 2010).

- In emergency/urgent cases where there is insufficient time to obtain prior consent, the instructing party must apply forthwith on notice for directions as to the next steps regarding the expert, see PD 25A accompanying the FPR 2010.

- Preliminary enquiries may be necessary in order to select the right expert. An approach to an expert should comply with PD 25A accompanying the FPR 2010. The instructing solicitor should then draft a proposed instruction in compliance and file it. Once it is agreed and leave is granted, it should be sent out within five days, PD 25A, paragraph 4.5.

- Obtain consents from the child and those with parental responsibility for examinations and assessments where appropriate (see Chapters 3 and 12).

- Discuss instruction of expert with other parties and try to agree joint experts wherever possible.

- The expert has an overriding duty to the court that takes precedence over the interests of any party, rule 25.3 of the FPR 2010 and the accompanying PD 25A.

- Directions of the court should be obtained for:
    - the date by which the letter of instruction should be sent;
    - documents to be released;
    - a date for filing the report.
- Examination of a child may require directions as to venue, timing, the person(s) to accompany the child and to whom the results should be given.

Letters of instruction

Should comply with PD 25A, paragraph 4.5 accompanying the FPR 2010. In brief, to:

- set out the context in which expert opinion sought;
- define specific questions the expert is to address;
- list the documentation provided or refer to a paginated bundle;
- identify materials that have not been produced either as original medical or other professional records or documents filed in response to an instruction from a party;
- identify all requests to third parties for information and responses;
- identify all the people concerned with the proceedings, informing the expert of his or her right to talk to them, provided an accurate record is made of discussions;
- identify any other expert instructed;
- define the contractual basis upon which the expert is instructed, including funding and payment details.

Letters of instruction should also be accompanied by a chronology with the background information, and request the expert to ask for further information or documentation if necessary.

The letter should then be filed at court with list of accompanying documents, and served on other parties unless the court otherwise directs.

Joint instructions are desirable, and can be directed by the court under rule 25.7 of the FPR 2010. Where joint letters of instruction are to be settled, see rule 25.8 and the accompanying PD 25A, paragraph 4.6.

It is very important to remember that any delay in sending out the letter of instruction to the expert is likely to compromise the ability of the expert to file his or her report by the filing deadline. This then leads to delay to the overall court timetable, which can result in delays of many weeks.

Updating, expert conferences, agreed evidence and points in issue

- Experts should be kept up to date with new documents filed in the case, PD 25A, paragraph 4.7 accompanying the FPR 2010.

- Experts may be invited to confer together, identifying areas of agreement and disputed issues. The court should regulate such meetings, PD 25A, paragraphs 6.3–6.5 accompanying the FPR 2010.

Expert reports

- Expert reports should be objective – the expert's overriding duty is to the court.

- Parties and lawyers should not attempt to influence or 'edit' expert reports.

- Reports must be disclosed to the court and to all parties unless otherwise directed by the court.

- The requirements for the content and ordering of an expert report are set out in PD 25A, paragraph 3.3 accompanying the FPR 2010.

- The expert report shall end with statements that:

    - the expert understands his or her duty to the court and will comply with it;

    - the expert does not consider that there is any conflict of interest, nor any interest disclosed that affects his or her suitability as an expert witness. The expert will advise those instructing him or her if there is any change in circumstances affecting the expert's answers regarding interests and suitability.

- The report shall end with a statement of truth as follows, see PD 25A accompanying the FPR 2010:

    I confirm that I have made clear which facts and matters referred to in this report are within my own knowledge and which are not. Those that are within my own knowledge I confirm to be true. The opinions I have expressed represent my true and complete professional opinions on the matters to which they refer.

18.4   Expert evidence in court

With careful planning by advocates, the time and patience of expert witnesses can be saved considerably. Joint consultations and jointly compiled experts' lists of agreed and disputed issues save time, whilst arrangement of evidence in a logical sequence to fit the needs of witnesses and the run of the evidence is vital. Written evidence can be admitted by agreement, and expert witnesses' time saved by reduction of their evidence in chief and more time in cross examination.

In Part 35 of the Civil Procedure Rules 1998, SI 1998/3132, the primary duty of an expert is stated to be to the court. Although it was the expectation of the courts, this duty did not specifically apply in family cases until 1 April 2008, when *Practice Direction: Experts in Family Proceedings Relating to Children*, 13 February, 2008, paragraph 3.1 came into effect. Now, that overriding duty to the court is very clearly stated in FPR 2010 and the accompanying PD 25A, paragraph 3.1.

Experts should never go beyond the remit of their instructions or their expertise. There have been cases in which, regrettably, this has happened, to the detriment of a party, the child, justice or possibly all three. The Court of Appeal gave helpful guidance for experts and lawyers in *R v Cannings* [2004] EWCA Crim 1, [2004] 1 WLR 2607.

18.5   Finances for expert evidence

Under the FPR 2010 and the accompanying PD 25A the contractual basis for the expert evidence, including funding and payment, should be set out in the letter of instruction.

Private funding is a matter of negotiation between client, solicitor and expert.

In publicly funded cases, the LSC places limitations on funding. High cost cases (lawyers are advised to check the current limit) are dealt with by the Special Cases Unit and the lawyer needs to present and justify an overall cost case plan.

Careful negotiation of expert fees is required in advance of the case to obtain prior authority for instruction of the expert.

Any additional unforeseen expense in respect of the expert's assessment or report preparation which arises after the initial authority must be addressed by an increase in any limitation on costs that has been imposed by the LSC.

Experts in publicly funded cases would be wise to accept instructions and begin work only when their fee structure, an estimate of their costs, and the responsibility for who will pay, along with an agreement as to how and when payment will be made, has been clarified. This contractual arrangement should be reflected in the letter of instruction,

When the expert's evidence or other work is concluded, claims for payment on account for expert services can be submitted to the LSC in advance of the final detailed assessment of the costs of the case (formerly called taxation).

Experts should be aware that, if the matter is publicly funded, in county court or High Court cases, the detailed assessment (new form of taxation) may, in some circumstances, lead to a reduction in the fees allowed for the expert's work.

18.6 Finding the right expert

The most effective way of finding experts is by personal recommendation by other legal practitioners in similar fields of practice. Children and Family Court Advisory and Support Service (CAFCASS), children's guardians, social workers, local authority lawyers and other professionals may also provide recommendations for experts in particular specialist areas. Expert(s) should be asked to disclose qualifications, current work and relevant past experience – not only for reassurance, but also because to do so is useful for the court, other parties and the LSC. The expert should be asked how often he or she has given evidence in court before; the expert may be absolutely brilliant on paper, but terrible at giving oral evidence.

The sources below may be a starting point in the search for the right expert. Some organisations will send out published lists, while others provide information in response to a telephone or written enquiry, and may charge an administration fee.

18.6.1 Registers, directories and lists

British Academy of Experts, *Register of Experts*.

British Psychological Society, *Directory of Chartered Psychologists*.

Forensic Science Society, *Register of Independent Consultants*.

Forensic Science Society, *World List of Forensic Science Laboratories and Practices*.

JS Publications, *UK Register of Expert Witnesses.*

Law Society, *Expert Witness Register.*

Law Society of Scotland, *Directory of Expert Witnesses.*

18.6.2   Online resources

British Psychological Society, www.bps.org.uk.

Expert Witness, www.expertwitness.co.uk.

Law Society of Scotland (Directory of Expert Witnesses), www.expertwitnessscotland.info/home.htm.

Legal Hub (Expert Witness Directory), www.legalhub.co.uk.

NAGALRO (Professional Association for Children's Guardians, Family Court Advisers and Independent Social Workers), www.nagalro.com.

UK Register of Expert Witnesses, www.jspubs.com.

18.6.3   Journals and supplements

Expert Evidence (The International Journal of Behavioural Science in Legal Contexts).

Law Society Gazette, Expert Witness Supplement.

Solicitors Journal, Expert Witnesses Supplement.

18.6.4   Lawyers' lists

Association of Lawyers for Children, Experts Database.

Law Society, Children Panel Membership List.

London Criminal Courts Solicitors' Association, Membership Directory.

18.6.5   Useful information on instructing experts

Children Act Advisory Committee, *Handbook of Best Practice in Children Act Cases* (HMSO/DoH, 1997).

Cowan, S and Hunt, AC, (2008) *Mason's Forensic Medicine for Lawyers* (Tottel, 5th edn, 2008).

Expert Witness Group, *Expert Witness Pack for Use in Children Act Proceedings* (Family Law, 1997).

Hodgkinson, T and James, M, *Expert Evidence Law and Practice* (Sweet & Maxwell, 2nd edn, 2006).

Kennedy, I and Grubb, A, *Medical Law: Text with Materials* (Oxford University Press, 3rd edn, 2000).

Wall, The Rt Hon Lord Justice and Hamilton, I, *A Handbook for Expert Witnesses in Children Act Cases* (Family Law, 2nd edn, 2007).

19 Sources and Guidance

19.1 Statutes

Abortion Act 1967.

Access to Health Records Act 1990.

Access to Justice Act 1999.

Access to Medical Reports Act 1988.

Adoption and Children Act 2002.

Adoption and Children (Scotland) Act 2007.

Care Standards Act 2000.

Carers and Disabled Children Act 2000.

Child Abduction Act 1984.

Child Abduction and Custody Act 1985.

Child Support Act 1991.

Children Act 1989.

Children Act 2004.

Children and Adoption Act 2006.

Children and Young Persons Act 1933.

Children and Young Persons Act 1969.

Children and Young Persons Act 2008.

Children (Leaving Care) Act 2000.

Children (Scotland) Act 1995.

Commissioner for Children and Young People (Scotland) Act 2003.

County Courts Act 1984.

Crime and Disorder Act 1998.

Data Protection Act 1988.

Domestic Proceedings and Magistrates' Courts Act 1978.

Domestic Violence Crime and Victims Act 2004.

Domicile and Matrimonial Proceedings Act 1973.

Education Act 2002.

Family Law Act 1986.

Family Law Act 1996.

Family Law Reform Act 1969.

Family Law Reform Act 1987.

Human Fertilisation and Embryology Act 1990.

Human Fertilisation and Embryology Act 2008.

Human Rights Act 1998.

Local Authority Social Services Act 1970.

Matrimonial and Family Proceedings Act 1984.

Mental Capacity Act 2005.

Mental Health Act 1983.

Police and Criminal Evidence Act 1984.

Protection from Harassment Act 1997.

Protection of Children Act 1999.

Race Relations Act 1976.

Rehabilitation of Offenders Act 1974.

Sexual Offences Act 1956.

Sexual Offences Act 2003.

Supreme Court Act 1981.

Surrogacy Arrangements Act 1985.

19.2   Statutory instruments

Access to Justice (Destination of Appeals) (Family Proceedings) Order 2009, SI 2009/871.

Access to Personal Files (Social Services) (Amendment) Regulations 1991, SI 1991/1587.

Access to Personal Files (Social Services) Regulations 1989, SI 1989/206.

Adoption Agencies Regulations 2005, SI 2005/389.

Adoption Agencies (Wales) Regulations 2005, SI 2005/1313.

Adoption (Bringing Children into the United Kingdom) Regulations 2003, SI 2003 /1173.

Adoption Information and Intermediary Services Regulations (pre-commencement) 2005, SI 2005/890.

Adoption Support Agencies (England) and Adoption Agencies (Miscellaneous Amendments) Regulations 2005, SI 2005/2720.

Adoption Support Services Regulations 2005, SI 2005/691.

Adoptions with a Foreign Element Regulations 2005, SI 2002/392.

Allocation and Transfer of Proceedings Order 2008, SI 2008/28.

Arrangements for Placement of Children (General) Regulations 1991, SI 1991/890.

Blood Tests (Evidence of Paternity) Regulations 1971, SI 1971/1861.

Care Homes Regulations 2001, SI 2001/3965.

Care Planning, Placement and Case Review Regulations 2010, SI 2010/959.

Child Minding and Day Care (Applications for Registration) (England) Regulations 2001, SI 2002/1829.

Child Minding and Day Care (Certificates of Registration) (England) Regulations 2001, SI 2001/1830.

Child Minding and Day Care (Suspension of Registration) (England) Regulations 2003, SI 2003/332.

Children Act 2004 (Children's Services) Regulations 2005, SI 2005/1972.

Children Act 2004 Information Database (England) Regulations 2007, SI 2007/2182.

Children (Admissibility of Hearsay Evidence) Order 1993, SI 1993/621.

Children (Allocation of Proceedings) Order 1991, SI 1991/1677.

Children (Allocation of Proceedings, Appeals) Order 1991, SI 1991/1801.

Children (Allocation of Proceedings) (Amendment) Order 1994, SI 1994/2164.

Children (Allocation of Proceedings) (Amendment) Order 1997, SI 1997/1897.

Children (Allocation of Proceedings) (Amendment) Order 1998, SI 1998/2166.

Children and Family Court Advisory and Support Service (Conduct of Litigation and Exercise of Rights of Audience) Regulations 2001, SI 2001/669.

Children (Leaving Care) (England) Regulations 2001, SI 2001/2874.

Children (Leaving Care) (Wales) Regulations 2001, SI 2001/2189.

Children (Private Arrangements for Fostering) Regulations 2005, SI 2005/1533.

Children (Private Arrangements for Fostering) (Wales) Regulations 2006, SI 2006/940.

Children (Secure Accommodation) Regulations 1991, SI 1991/1505.

Children (Secure Accommodation No 2) Regulations 1991, SI 1991/2034.

Civil Procedure Rules 1998, SI 1998/3132.

Community Legal Service (Cost Protection) Regulations 2000, SI 2000/824.

Community Legal Service (Costs) Regulations 2000, SI 2000/441.

Community Legal Service (Financial Regulations) 2000, SI 2000/516.

Contact with Children Regulations 1991, SI 1991/891.

County Court Rules 1981, SI 1981/1687.

Court of Protection Rules 2007, SI 2007/1744.

Data Protection (Processing of Sensitive Personal Data) Order 2000, SI 2000/417.

Data Protection (Subject Access Modification) (Social Work) Order 2000, SI 2000/415.

Disclosure of Adoption Information (Post-Commencement Adoptions) Regulations 2005, SI 2005/888.

Disqualification from Caring for Children Regulations 2002, SI 2002/635.

Family Law Act 1996 (Part IV) (Allocation of Proceedings) Order 1997, SI 1997/1896.

Family Procedure (Adoption) Rules 2005, SI 2005/2795.

Family Procedure Rules 2010, SI 2010/2955 (and accompanying Practice Directions).

Family Proceedings Courts (Children Act 1989) Rules 1991, SI 1991/1395.

Fostering Services Regulations 2002, SI 2002/57.

Foster Placement (Children) Regulations 1991, SI 1991/910.

Guardians ad Litem and Reporting Officers (Panels) (Amendment) Regulations 1997, SI 1997/1662.

Parental Responsibility Agreement (Amendment) Regulations 1994, SI 1994/3157.

Parental Responsibility Agreement Regulations 1991, SI 1991/1478.

Placement of Children with Parents etc Regulations 1991, SI 1991/893.

Representations Procedure (Children) Regulations 1991, SI 1991/894.

Review of Children's Cases Regulations 1991, SI 1991/895.

Rules of the Supreme Court 1965, SI 1965/1776.

Special Guardianship Regulations 2005, SI 2005/1109.

Special Guardianship (Wales) Regulations 2005, SI 2005/1513.

Suitability of Adopters Regulations 2005, SI 2002/1712.

19.3   Conventions and Protocols

European Convention for the Protection of Human Rights and Fundamental Freedoms 1950.

Protocols made under the European Convention for the Protection of Human Rights and Fundamental Freedoms 1950.

UN Convention on the Rights of the Child.

19.4   President's Guidance

Adopted Children Register: Restriction on Disclosure [1999] 1 FLR 315.

Practice Direction: Guide to Case Management in Public Law Proceedings, 1 April 2008.

Practice Direction: Public Law Proceedings Guide to Case Management, April 2010.

President's Guidance: Adoption Proceedings. Intercountry Adoption Centres, December 2007.

President's Guidance: Adoption: The New Law and Procedure, March 2006.

President's Guidance: Communicating with the Home Office in Family Proceedings, October 2010.

President's Guidance in Relation to Split Hearings [2010] 2 FCR 271.

President's Guidance: Out of Hours Hearings, 18 November 2010.

19.5   Government and Law Society publications

19.5.1   General sources

UK Government publications are available from The Stationery Office (TSO), PO Box 29, Norwich NR3 1GN, 0870 600 5522, www.tsoshop.co.uk, customer.services@tso.co.uk.

* The Department for Education (formerly the Department for Children Schools and Families) publishes policy regarding children's services in England, www.education.gov.uk.

* The Ministry of Justice publishes policy regarding the courts in England and Wales, www.justice.gov.uk.

The Scottish Office and The Scottish Executive publications are available at www.scotland.gov.uk. See also Scottish Courts, www.scotcourts.gov.uk.

The Welsh Government publishes policy regarding children's services in Wales, www.wales.gov.uk.

19.5.2   Publications

UK

Acting for Children (Law Society, 1992).

Acting in the Absence of a Children's Guardian (Law Society, 2009).

Appointing a Solicitor for the Child in Specified Proceedings: Guidelines for Courts (Law Society, 2007).

Assessing Children in Need and their Families: Practice Guidance (DoH, 2000)

Best Practice Guide – Preparing for Care and Supervision Proceedings (Ministry of Justice, 2009), www.justice.gov.uk.

Centile charts for baby growth, with accompanying explanatory notes (obtainable from a GP or health visitor and at www.gp-training.net).

Confidentiality: NHS Code of Practice (DoH, 2003).

Every Child Matters: Change for Children (DfES, 2004), www.education.gov.uk.

Family Assessment Pack of Questionnaires and Scales (DoH, 2000).

Family Justice Review Final Report (Ministry of Justice, 2011).

Family Law Protocol (Law Society, 2006).

Framework for the assessment of children in need and their families (DoH, 2000).

Guidelines for Judges Meeting Children who are subject to Family Proceedings (Family Justice Council, April 2010).

Handbook of Best Practice in Children Act Cases (Children Act Advisory Committee, 1997).

Information Sharing – A Practitioner's Guide (DfES, 2006).

Initial and Core Assessment Records (DoH, 2000)

Introduction to the Children Act 1989 (DoH, 1991).

IRO Handbook: Statutory guidance for independent reviewing officers and local authorities on their functions in relation to case management and review for looked after children (DfE, 2010).

Local Safeguarding Children Board Manual (formerly the *ACPC Local Manual*). If available, usually obtainable from the LSCB Chair, there may be a fee payable.

Making Arrangements to Safeguard and Promote the Welfare of Children (DfES, 2005).

Protecting Children: A Guide to Social Workers Undertaking a Comprehensive Assessment (DoH, 1988).

Putting Care into Practice; Statutory Guidance for Local Authorities in Care Planning, Placement and Case Review for Looked after Children (DfE, 2010).

Report of the Inquiry into Child Abuse in Cleveland (HMSO, 1987).

Representation of Children in Public Law Proceedings (Law Society, 2006).

Safeguarding Children and Young People who may be Affected by Gang Activity (DCSF, 2010).

Safeguarding children who may have been trafficked – Practice guidance (DCSF, 2011).

Statutory guidance on the roles and responsibilities of the Director of Children's Services and the Lead Member for Children's Services (DfE, 2012).

The Children Act 1989 Guidance and Regulations (DCSF). Issued in ten volumes, revised at various times, comprising:

- Volume 1 *Court Orders (England)* (revised 2008)
- Volume 1 *Court Orders (Wales)* (2008)
- Volume 2 *Family Support, Day Care, and Educational Provision for Young Children* (1991)
- Volume 3 *Family Placements* (1991) (no longer available)
- Volume 4 *Residential Care* (1991)
- Volume 5 *Independent Schools* (1991)
- Volume 6 *Children with Disabilities* (1991, 4th impression 1999)
- Volume 7 *Guardians ad Litem and Other Court Related Issues (1991)* (replaced by CAFCASS policies)
- Volume 8 *Private Fostering and Miscellaneous* (1991)
- Volume 9 *Adoption Issues* (3rd impression 2002)
- Volume 10 *Index* (1992)

The Care of Children, Principles and Practice in Regulations and Guidance (DoH, 1991).

The Child's World, Assessing Children in Need, Training and Development Pack (DoH, 2000).

The Funding Code (Legal Services Commission, 2011).

The Good Practice Guide in Child Care Cases (The Law Society, 2010).

The Protection of Children in England: A Progress Report (TSO, 2009).

The SFLA Guide to Good Practice for Solicitors Acting for Children (SFLA, 6th edn, 2002).

The Victoria Climbié Inquiry: Report (TSO, 2003).

What To Do if You're Worried a Child is being Abused (DfES, 2006).

Working Together to Safeguard Children: A guide to inter-agency working to safeguard and promote the welfare of children (DCSF, 2010) (watch for a new edition).

Northern Ireland

Children Order Advisory Committee – Best Practice Guidance (DHSSPSNI, 2003).

Scotland

Framework for Standards and Children's Charter (Scottish Executive, 2003).

Getting it Right for Every Child (Scottish Executive, 2006).

Getting our Priorities Right (Scottish Executive, 2002).

"It's Everyone's Job to Make Sure I'm Alright": Report of the Child Protection Audit and Review (Scottish Executive, 2003).

Protecting Children and Young People: The Charter (Scottish Executive, 2004).

Protecting Children and Young People: The Framework for Standards (Scottish Executive, 2004).

Protecting Children – A shared responsibility. Guidance for Health Professionals in Scotland (Scottish Office, 1998).

Protecting Children – A shared responsibility – Guidance on Inter-Agency Co-operation (Scottish Office, 1998).

Sharing Information about Children at Risk (Scottish Executive, 2003).

19.6 Home Office and Local Authority Circulars

Home Office Circular 88/1982.

Home Office Circular 105/1982.

Home Office Circular 102/1988.

Home Office Circular 45/1991.

Local Authority Circular LAC (88)20.

Local Authority Circular LAC (98)29.

Local Authority Circular LAC (99)29.

19.7 Reading and reference list

This list includes references cited in the text and additional publications recommended by practitioners as useful resource material for child law practitioners.

19.7.1 Looseleaf reference works

Hershman, D and McFarlane, A (eds), *Children Law and Practice* (Family Law).

Jones, RM (ed), *The Encyclopaedia of Social Services and Child Care Law* (Sweet & Maxwell).

Sax, R et al, *The Family Law Service* (Butterworths).

White, R and others (ed), *Clarke Hall and Morrison on Children* (Butterworths).

19.7.2 Books and research

Barker, J and Hodes, D, *The Child in Mind: A Child Protection Handbook* (Routledge, 3rd edn, 2007).

Bedingfield, D, *Advocacy in Family Proceedings* (Jordan Publishing, 2012).

Bentovim, A and Bingley Miller, L, *The Family Assessment of Family Competence, Strengths and Difficulties* (Brighton Publishing, 2001).

Brandon, M, Belderson, P, et al, *Analysing Child Deaths and Serious Injury through Abuse and Neglect: What can we Learn? – A Biennial Analysis of Serious Case Reviews 2003 – 2005* (DCSF, 2008).

Brophy, J, et al, 'The Contribution of Experts in Care Proceedings: Evaluation of Independent Social Work Reports in Care Proceedings' (Oxford University, 2012).

Calder, MC, *Contemporary Risk Assessment in Safeguarding Children* (Russell House, 2008).

Charlesworth, R, *Understanding Child Development* (Delmar Learning, 2003).

Cox, A and Walker, S, *The HOME Inventory – Home Observation and Measurement of the Environment* (Pavilion Publishing, 2002).

Dent, H and Flynn, R. (eds), *Children as Witnesses* (Wiley, 1996).

Department of Health and Social Services Inspectorate, *The Right to Complain* (HMSO, 1991).

Expert Witness Group, *Expert Witness Pack for Use in Children Act Proceedings* (Family Law, 1997).

Family Justice Council, *Parents who lack capacity to conduct public law proceedings* (Family Justice Council, 2010), available at www.judiciary.gov.uk.

Farmer, R and Moyers, S, *Kinship Care: Fostering Effective Family and Friends Placements* (Jessica Kingsley, 2008).

Fordham, M, *Judicial Review Case Studies* (Hart Publishing, 5th edn, 2008).

Fordham, M, *Judicial Review Handbook* (Hart Publishing, 5th edn, 2008).

Fortin, J, *Children's Rights and the Developing Law* (Cambridge University Press, 2009).

Friel, J, *Children with Special Needs* (Jessica Kingsley, 4th edn, 1997).

General Medical Council, *Consent guidance: patients and doctors making decisions together* (General Medical Council, 2008), available at www.gmc-uk.org.

Goldthorpe, L and Monro, P, *Child Law Handbook: Guide to good practice* (Law Society, 2005).

Hobart, C. and Frankel, J, *A Practical Guide to Child Observation and Assessment* (Nelson Thornes, 2004).

Holt, KS, *Child Development – Diagnosis and Assessment* (Butterworths, 1994).

Howarth, J (ed.), *The Child's World: The Comprehensive Guide to Assessing Children in Need,* (Jessica Kingsley, 2nd edn, 2010).

Hunt, J, Waterhouse, S and Lutman, E, *Keeping Them in the Family: Outcomes for children placed in kinship care through care proceedings* (BAAF, 2008).

Isaacs, E and Shepherd, C, *Social Work Decision Making: A guide for child care lawyers* (Family Law, 2012).

Mahendra, B, *Risk Assessment in Psychiatry* (Family Law, 2008).

Manning, J, *Judicial Review Proceedings* (LAG, 2nd edn, 2004).

McFarlane, A and Reardon, M, *Child Care and Adoption Law* (Family Law, 2010).

Megitt, C, *Child Development: An Illustrated Guide* (Heinemann, 2nd edn, 2006).

Monro, P and Forrester, P, *The Children's Guardian* (Publisher, 1995).

Pressdee, P, Vater, J, Judd, F and Baker, J, *The Public Law Outline: The Court Companion*, (Family Law, 2008).

Reder, P, Duncan, S and Gray, M, *Beyond Blame* (Routledge, 1993).

Rose, W and Barnes, J, *Improving Safeguarding Practice – Study of Serious Case Reviews 2001 – 2003* (DCSF, 2008).

Royal College of Paediatrics and Child Health, Royal College of Physicians of London and its Faculty of Forensic and Legal Medicine, *The Physical Signs of Child Sexual Abuse: An evidence-based review and guidance for best practice* (RCPCH, 2008).

Taylor, C, *Improving Attendance at School* (DfE, 2012).

Timms, JE, *Children's Representation, A Practitioner's Guide* (Sweet & Maxwell, 2003).

Valman, HB, *ABC of One to Seven* (British Medical Association, 4th edn, 1999).

Valman, HB, *Children's Medical Guide* (Dorling Kindersley Publishing, 1997).

Wall, Justice (ed), *Rooted Sorrows* (Family Law, 1997).

Wall, The Rt Hon Lord Justice and Hamilton, I, *A Handbook for Expert Witnesses in Children Act Cases* (Family Law, 2nd edn, 2007).

Wolanski, A and Wilson, K, *The Family Courts: Media Access & Reporting* (President of the Family Division, Judicial College, Society of Editors, 2011), available at www.judiciary.gov.uk.

19.7.3 Legal resources

British and Irish Legal Information Institute (BAILII) website publishes all High Court, Court of Appeal and Supreme Court judgments, www.bailii.org.

Care Council for Wales publishes *Child Law for Social Workers in Wales* in English and Welsh, with regular updates, www.ccwales.org.uk/child-law/.

Family Law Reports and *Family Law*, www.familylaw.co.uk.

Family Law Solicitors Guide/Family Law Directory, www.familylawdirectory.co.uk.

Family Law Week, www.familylawweek.co.uk.

Justis, www.justis.com.

Scottish Statutes and Statutory Instruments, www.legislation.gov.uk.

TSO online bookshop, www.tsoshop.co.uk.

UK Statutes and Statutory Instruments, www.legislation.gov.uk.

20 Improving Law, Skills and Practice

It is necessary for lawyers to keep up to date with statute and case law and to constantly develop knowledge and skills, not only in law but, for example, in medicine, psychology and parenting.

Look for training events which are accredited by the Solicitors Regulation Authority (courses which were formerly accredited by the Law Society), the Bar Council, or the Family Mediation Council and those run by the associations listed in para 20.1.

It is vital to maintain a list of resources to which child clients and families may be referred and it helps to belong to organisations which can provide information and assistance. In those areas of the country where child law practitioners may find themselves isolated, discussion with a network of colleagues provides moral and practical support.

20.1 Professional and interdisciplinary associations

Legal practitioners are represented on the local Family Justice Councils, which are interdisciplinary groups attached to each care centre, shortly to be replaced by local Family Justice Boards.

A good resource for child law practice is the experience of colleagues. Listed below are some of the organisations which have been recommended to us as helpful in the provision of networking, training and information. By listing these, we are not expressing any preference, and the list is by no means exhaustive.

Association of Lawyers for Children (ALC), PO Box 283, East Molesey, KT8 0WH, 020 8224 7071, www.alc.org.uk, admin@alc.org.uk.

British Association for Adoption and Fostering (BAAF), Saffron House, 6–10 Kirby Street, London EC1N 8TS, 020 7421 2600, fax: 020 7421 2601, www.baaf.org.uk, mail@baaf.org.uk.

British Association for the Study and Prevention of Child Abuse and Neglect (BASPCAN), 17 Priory Street, York YO1 6ET, 01904 613605, fax: 01904 642239, www.baspcan.org.uk, baspcan@baspcan.org.uk.

Children and Family Court Advisory and Support Service (CAFCASS), 6th Floor, Sanctuary Buildings, Great Smith Street, London SW1P 3BT, 0844 353 3350, fax: 0844 353 3351, www.cafcass.gov.uk, webenquiries@cafcass.gsi.gov.uk.

Family Justice Council, www.judiciary.gov.uk/about-the-judiciary/advisory-bodies/fjc/index.

Judicial College (judicial training, formerly the remit of the Judicial Studies Board). Publications and useful information are available at www.judiciary.gov.uk.

Local Children's Guardian and Solicitor Groups: check with local CAFCASS managers.

NAGALRO (Professional Association for Children's Guardians, Family Court Advisers and Independent Social Workers), PO Box 264, Esher, Surrey KT10 0WA, 01372 818504, fax: 01372 818505, www.nagalro.com, nagalro@globalnet.co.uk. (Note: NAGALRO has a great Google group for practitioners – membership is available to child and family lawyers.)

National Youth Advisory Service (NYAS), Egerton House, Tower Road, Birkenhead, Wirral CH41 1FN, 0151 649 8700, fax: 0151 649 8701, www.nyas.net, main@nyas.net.

Resolution, Central Office, PO Box 302, Orpington, Kent BR6 8QX, 01689 820272, fax: 01689 896972, www.resolution.org.uk, info@resolution.org.uk.

20.2   The Law Society's Children Panel

The Children Panel comprises practitioners specialising in the representation of children, families and local authorities in public or private law matters.

For membership, applicants must have post-qualification experience in child and family law and a sound knowledge of child law and practice. In addition, they need an understanding of child-related issues, for example, child development, attachment and separation, recognition of child abuse, contact and care planning. They also need to develop their skills in communicating with children.

Solicitors wishing to be accepted for membership of the Children Panel must produce evidence of the appropriate qualifications and relevant experience, provide references, acquire the necessary training and, on application, will be asked to submit written answers to questions. Lastly, they must pass a selection interview.

Children Panel training courses are comprehensive, covering a wide range of topics and law relevant to the representation of children, families and local authorities and working with the children's guardian.

Information about the Children Panel and application forms can be obtained from The Solicitors Regulation Authority, Ipsley Court, Berrington Close, Redditch, Worcestershire B98 0TD, DX 19114 Redditch, www.sra.org.uk, contactcentre@sra.org.uk.

20.3 Sources of useful information and contacts for children and families, and those who work with them

ChildLine, 0800 1111, www.childline.org.uk.

Churches Child Protection Advisory Service, www.ccpas.co.uk.

Community Care, www.communitycare.co.uk.

CORAM Children's Legal Centre, Child Protection Project, www.protectingchildren.org.uk, 01207 713 0089, cpp@essex.ac.uk, free legal advice for professionals 0207 636 1245. The Child Protection Project launched in 2012 and is designed for the provision of legal information and advice on child protection and safeguarding issues to frontline practitioners.

Family Law Week, www.familylawweek.co.uk (legal updates on family law).

General Medical Council (GMC), www.gmc-uk.org (see child protection guidance for doctors).

Government information, www.direct.gov.uk. See also the beta website www.gov.uk in the process of trial.

Northern Ireland government guidance, www.dhsspsni.gov.uk.

NSPCC, www.nspcc.org.uk.

Scottish Child Law Centre, www.sclc.org.uk.

Scottish Government guidance www.scotland.gov.uk.

Welsh Government guidance, http://wales.gov.uk.